THE MYSTICS OF SPAIN

ETHICAL AND RELIGIOUS CLASSICS

RŪMĪ : POET AND MYSTIC
Translated with Introduction and Notes
by Reynold A. Nicholson

SUFISM
by A. J. Arberry

.THE POETRY AND CAREER OF LIPO
by Arthur Waley

ST. FRANCIS IN ITALIAN PAINTING
by George Kaftal

GENERAL EDITORS
A. J. ARBERRY, S. RADHAKRISHNAN, H. N. SPALDING AND
F. W. THOMAS

ETHICAL AND RELIGIOUS CLASSICS
OF THE EAST AND WEST
NO. 5

THE MYSTICS OF SPAIN

by E. Allison Peers

THE MYSTICS
OF SPAIN

By

E. ALLISON PEERS

LONDON

GEORGE ALLEN & UNWIN LTD

Ruskin House Museum Street

GENERAL INTRODUCTION

As a result of two Wars that have devastated the world men and women everywhere feel a twofold need. We need a deeper understanding and appreciation of other peoples and their civilizations, especially their moral and spiritual achievements. And we need a new vision of the Universe, a clearer insight into the fundamentals of ethics and religion. How ought men to behave? How ought nations? Does God exist? What is His Nature? How is He related to His creation? Especially, how can man approach Him? In other words, there is a general desire to know what the greatest minds, whether of East or West, have thought and said about the Truth of God and of the beings who (as most of them hold) have sprung from Him, live by Him, and return to Him.

It is the object of this Series, which originated among a group of Oxford men and their friends, to place the chief ethical and religious masterpieces of the world, both Christian and non-Christian, within easy reach of the intelligent reader who is not an expert—the undergraduate, the ex-Service man who is interested in the East, the adult student, the intelligent public generally. The Series will contain books of three kinds: translations, reproductions of ethical and religious art, and Background Books showing the surroundings in which the literature and art arose and developed. These books overlap each other. Religious art, both in East and West, often illustrates a religious text, and in suitable cases the text and pictures will be printed together to complete each other. The Background Books will often consist largely of translations. The volumes will be prepared by scholars of distinction, who will try to make them, not only scholarly, but intelligible and enjoyable.

Their contents will also be very varied—ethical and social, biographical, devotional, philosophic and mystical,

7

whether in poetry, in pictures or in prose. There is a great wealth of material. Confucius lived in a time much like our own, when State was at war with State and the people suffering and disillusioned; and the Classics he preserved or inspired show the social virtues that may unite families, classes and States into one great family, in obedience to the Will of Heaven. Asoka and Akbar (both of them great patrons of art) ruled a vast Empire on the principles of religious faith. There are the moral anecdotes and moral maxims of the Jewish and Muslim writers of the Middle Ages. There are the beautiful tales of courage, love and fidelity in the Indian and Persian epics. Shakespeare's plays show that he thought the true relation between man and man is love. Here and there a volume will illustrate the unethical or less ethical man and the difficulties that beset him.

Then there are the devotional and philosophic works. The lives and legends (legends often express religious truth with clarity and beauty) of the Buddha, of the parents of Mary, of Francis of Assisi, and the exquisite sculptures and paintings that illustrate them. Indian and Christian religious music, and the words of prayer and praise which the music intensifies. There are the Prophets and Apocalyptic writers, Zarathustrian and Hebrew; the Greek philosophers and the Christian thinkers—Greek, Latin, Medieval and Modern—whom they so deeply influenced. There is too the Hindu, Buddhist and Christian teaching expressed in such great monuments as the Indian temples, Barabudur (the Chartres of Asia), and Ajanta, Chartres itself and the Sistine Chapel.

Finally there are the mystics of feeling, and the mystical philosophers. In God-loving India the poets, musicians, sculptors and painters inspired by the spiritual worship of Krishna and Rama, as well as the philosophic mystics from the Upanishads onwards. The two great Taoists, Lao-tze and Chuang-tze and the Sung mystical painters in China, Rūmi and other Sūfis in Islam, Plato and Plotinus, followed by 'Dionysius,' Dante, Eckhart, Teresa and other great mystics and mystical painters in many Christian lands.

Mankind is hungry, but the feast is there, though it is locked up and hidden away. It is the aim of this Series to put it within reach, so that, like the heroes of Homer, we may stretch out our hands to the good cheer laid before us.

No doubt the great religions differ in fundamental respects. But they are not nearly so far from one another as they seem. We think they are further off than they are largely because we so often misunderstand and misrepresent them. Those whose own religion is dogmatic have often been as ready to learn from other teachings as those who are liberals in religion. Above all there is an enormous amount of common ground in the great religions, concerning too the most fundamental matters. There is frequent agreement on the Divine Nature; God is the One, Self-Subsisting Reality, knowing Himself, and therefore loving and rejoicing in Himself. Nature and finite spirits are in some way subordinate kinds of Being, or merely appearances of the Divine, the One. The Way of man's approach or return to God is in essence the same, in Christian and in non-Christian teaching. It has three stages: an ethical stage, then one of knowledge and love, leading to the mystical Union of the soul with God. Each stage will be illustrated in these volumes.

Something of all this may (it is hoped) be learnt from the books and pictures in this Series. Read and pondered with a desire to learn, they will help men and women to find fullness of life, and peoples to live together in greater understanding and harmony. To-day the earth is beautiful, but men are disillusioned and afraid. But there will come a day, perhaps not a distant day, when there will be a Renaissance of man's spirit: when men will be innocent and happy amid the beauty of the world. For their eyes will be opened to see that egoism and strife are folly, that the Universe is Spiritual, and that men are the sons of God.

They shall not hurt nor destroy
In all my holy mountain:
For all the earth shall be full of the knowledge
    of the Lord
As the waters cover the sea.

PREFACE

With a few outstanding exceptions, the treasures of Spanish mysticism have lain in oblivion for three centuries, their greatness unsuspected even in Spain itself. The aim of this book is to present a general survey of the Golden Age of Spanish mysticism as a background to the works and personalities of fifteen mystical authors, represented by short extracts from their writings. Particulars of relevant, and accessible, editions and studies are prefaced to the selections from each author and a list of books somewhat wider in scope is provided for those who wish to make this anthology a starting-point for further study.

All the extracts have been translated specifically for this book with the exception of two poems which are reproduced, by permission of the publishers, from my *Poems of St. John of the Cross* (London, Burns Oates, 1947). I owe the warmest thanks to Messrs. Methuen & Co., publishers of *Spanish Mysticism: a Preliminary Survey*, the earliest book I wrote on this subject, for the readiness with which they granted me permission to incorporate some passages from it in the introduction to this volume.

E. A. P.

University of Liverpool.
February 9, 1950.

11

CONTENTS

[1] The authors excerpted are arranged in chronological order of the dates of their birth.

13

14

THE MYSTICS OF SPAIN

The remarkable florescence of ascetic and mystical literature in sixteenth- and seventeenth-century Spain is one of
the most striking phenomena in the history of Christian
devotion. Using the adjective 'mystical' in its widest sense,
the foremost Spanish critic of the nineteenth century, Mar-
celino Menéndez y Pelayo, computed that the number of
works—either published or still in manuscript—to which
it can be applied must be in the region of three thousand;
and even if we take the word in a more restricted sense it
is safe to assert that mystical authors who wrote during that
great age can be counted by the hundred.

I

Throughout the Middle Ages, which gave such notable
mystics to Italy, Germany, the Low Countries and England,
religious fervour in Spain was directed mainly to the task
of expelling the Moslems and thus winning back the whole
of the country for the Cross. But in the thirteenth century
one figure of distinction stands out—a Majorcan, Ramón
Lull. Converted, as a young man, from a life of ease and
dissipation, Lull devoted fifty years of a long life to mis-
sionary work among the heathen—and, in particular, among
the Moors. An indefatigable preacher, and a phenomenal
traveller, he was also a voluminous writer: though legend
has certainly fathered more treatises upon him than he
could ever have written, the total of his genuine works—
some in Latin, some in his native Catalan—can hardly be
less than two hundred and fifty. A considerable proportion
of these may be described as mystical in spirit—many of
his poems, large parts of his vast and encyclopædic *Book of
Contemplation*, passages from the religious romances, *Felix*
and *Blanquerna*, a few short treatises, of which the best

15

known is the *Art of Contemplation,* and a number of fantastic allegorical works, such as the *Tree of the Philosophy of Love.* But the opuscule which gives Lull's mysticism immortality is the unforgettable little *Book of the Lover and the Beloved.* In writing this, he tells us, he drew upon Moslem sources: 'certain men called Sufis' set down 'words of love and brief examples which give men great devotion; and these are words which demand exposition, and by the exposition thereof the understanding soars aloft, and the will likewise soars, and is increased in devotion.' [1] Under the essentially mystical figure of the Beloved —God—and His lover—the contemplative soul—Lull not only uses picturesque and appealing language to describe the Incarnation, the Passion and the Crucifixion of Christ, but points those who have fallen in love with God to the renunciations, the perils and the glories of the mystical life and to the sublimity of its goal. Across the centuries he still bids those who love come light their lanterns at his heart, and not only the ardour with which his memory is venerated by his own countrymen but the assiduity with which his little book is read in other languages than his own suggest that never have more of God's lovers responded to that appeal than do so to-day.

It was in about the year 1315 that Ramón Lull was martyred in North Africa, and two centuries were to pass before Spain—a newly united country—could produce a mystic of comparable stature. But when, in 1500, eight years after the completion of the Reconquest, Gómez García's *Chariot of the two lives* was published at Seville, those familiar with the mystical literature of other countries— and especially with Richard of St. Victor—must have realized that this picture contrasting the contemplative life with the active was introducing such literature into Spain. In the same year there appeared a much more original work, entitled the *Book of Exercises for the Spiritual Life.* Its author, a Benedictine, García de Cisneros, was an Abbot of Montserrat, who had gone to that famous house from

---

[1] BLANQUERNA, London, n.d. [1926], p. 410.

16

the Benedictine monastery at Valladolid to reform it, and the *Book of Exercises* was written for his own monks, in order to lay firm spiritual foundations on which his reforms were to be built. The goal it envisages is the goal of the mystic, 'the uniting of the soul with God,' and the exercises which comprise it are drawn up 'according to the three ways which are called Purgative, Illuminative and Unitive, to the end that, by means of the practice therof, and through prayer and contemplation, (the exercitant) may mount by ordered steps till he reach the desired end, which is the union of the soul with God.'[1] Though again and again surpassed in merit during the Golden Age of Spanish mysticism, it had a wide public, and by no means only a Benedictine one. During the sixteenth century, it went into five editions in Spanish, seven in Latin, two in Italian and one in French, and twentieth-century translators in English, French, German and Catalan testify to its continued vitality. This is partly due to the influence which it certainly had on St. Ignatius of Loyola, who no doubt first made its acquaintance at Montserrat or at Manresa. 'All we who are of the Society,' wrote St. Ignatius' contemporary biographer, Ribadeneira, 'must give thanks to our Lord that our blessed Father . . . found so good a confessor and profited by so good a book.' [2]

The life-story of St. Ignatius—converted at about the same age as Ramón Lull and in several ways curiously resembling him both in his temperament and in his later career[3]—is too well known to need re-telling here. It is difficult to assign to his *Spiritual Exercises* their exact place in this approximately chronological survey, since it was a work of gradual growth and the date of 1548 usually assigned to it is that of its first publication, in Latin, after the Pope had given it his formal approval. Before this event took place the Golden Age of mysticism in Spain had been initiated by a small but brilliant group of Franciscans.

[1] BOOK OF EXERCISES FOR THE SPIRITUAL LIFE, Montserrat, 1929, p. 45.
[2] STUDIES OF THE SPANISH MYSTICS, Vol. II, London, 1930, p. 34.
This book is referred to hereinafter as STUDIES.
[3] STUDIES, Vol. I, London, 1927, pp. 4-7.

Bernardino de Laredo, a doctor of medicine who entered the cloister at twenty-eight and spent thirty years as a lay brother in a friary near Seville, is remembered principally for a single mystical treatise, the *Ascent of Mount Sion*. Francisco de Osuna, also from the neighbourhood of Seville, wrote six ascetic and mystical works called *Spiritual Alphabets*, of which the *Third* has become famous. St. Peter of Alcántara, whose name is associated with the Discalced, or Barefooted, Reform in the Franciscan Order, was the author of 'several little books on prayer written in Spanish,'[1] the only one of which to have survived is the *Treatise of Prayer and Meditation*, translated into English, in 1632, as the 'Golden Treatise of Mental Prayer.'

These three mystics can be grouped together, not only because they wrote at approximately the same time and belonged to the same Order, but because they all influenced a much greater mystic, St. Teresa of Jesus. From Osuna's *Third Spiritual Alphabet*, which she first read when quite young, she learned something of the Prayer of Quiet. Laredo's treatise she lighted upon at a period of spiritual crisis and immediately recognized him as a fellow-traveller on the Mystic Way. St. Peter of Alcántara, whom she met a few years before his death, became her adviser in material as well as in spiritual matters, and she recommended his works for her nuns' reading.[2]

With these Franciscans may be grouped a number of other mystical writers who influenced her in various ways. To Luis de Granada, a Dominican, and a writer at once powerful and prolific, she wrote: 'I am one of the many people who love your Paternity in the Lord for the most holy and edifying doctrine which is in your writings.'[3] These, which are also prescribed for reading in her *Constitutions*, include the *Book of Prayer and Meditation* (1554), which in five years went into eleven editions; the *Sinners' Guide*

[1] COMPLETE WORKS OF ST. TERESA OF JESUS, London, 1946, Vol. I, p. 194.

[2] OP. CIT., Vol. III, p. 221.

[3] LETTERS OF ST. TERESA OF JESUS, London, 1951, p. 216.

(1567), his most popular book, but wholly ascetic; and the *Introduction to the Symbol of the Faith* (1582-3). Another of St. Teresa's advisers, Juan de Ávila, a secular priest known as the 'Apostle of Andalusia', wrote an early book entitled *Audi Filia* (1530), though the bulk of his output consists of sermons and a large number of spiritual letters. A much younger man from whom she learned was a disciple of her own, the Carmelite Jerónimo Gracián: her debt to him, however, was mainly personal, practically all his books (e.g., *The Burning Lamp*, 1586; *The Heavenly Road*, 1601, reissued as *Mystical Theology*, 1607; *Elucidation concerning the true spirit*, 1604; *Life of the Soul*, 1609; and the autobiographical *Pilgrimage of Anastasius*, 1613) being published after her death.

Before leaving this group we may refer to two Franciscan mystics somewhat later in date than those already mentioned. Diego de Estella, a pure ascetic in his *Book of the Vanity of the World* (1562), belongs to the history of mysticism by virtue of his *Devout Meditations on the love of God* (1576),which immediately after publication went into three more editions and is still being republished to-day. The *Meditations* are essentially a 'Book of the Lover and the Beloved'. Their author has 'fallen in love with God';[1] they have the formlessness and prolixity, as well as the sincerity and ardour, of a lover's outpourings, and it is by the lover that they will be most read.

Juan de los Ángeles, on the other hand, has often the precision of a scientist, and in him, better than in any of his contemporaries, may be studied the psychology of mysticism. The *Triumphs of the love of God* (1590), republished in enlarged form as *A Loving and Spiritual Strife between God and the soul* (1600), discusses the nature of love and three steps in the soul's mystical progress. The *Conquest of the Spiritual and Secret Kingdom of God* (1593) and its sequel, *Manual of the Perfect Life* (1608), both written in the form of dialogues between a friar and

---

[1] STUDIES, Vol. I, London, 1927, p. xiii.

his spiritual director, range widely over the field of mystical activity, dealing in especial detail with states and practices common to all mystical experience, such as introversion, recollection, contemplation and quiet, though it has also a great deal to say about the Dark Night of the Soul and about Union. The long, though incomplete, *Spiritual Considerations on the Song of Songs* (1607) has many passages dealing with the Mystic Way, though it says more of Purgation and Illumination than of Union.

Next come a group of Augustinian mystics, varying in type, as in merit, but all noteworthy, who between them more than cover the entire century. Alonso de Orozco, who was born in 1500, and lived to be ninety, almost spans it himself. His *Mount of Contemplation* (1544) describes the Mystic Way as a whole; the *Memorial of Holy Love* (1554), chiefly its lower stages. There are some glowing passages in his *History of the Queen of Sheba* (1565) and *The Sweetness of God* (1576) and also in the sermons and the minor works (among them a noteworthy commentary, the *Nine Names of Christ*) which he produced in such abundance. Cristóbal de Fonseca wrote toward the end of the century. His *Treatise on the love of God* (1592), of which eight editions were published before 1600, reveals him as a Platonist and a student of the pseudo-Dionysius. His other chief work, however, the *Life of Christ our Lord* (1596-1614), has little connection with mysticism. Another Platonist, Pedro Malón de Chaide, has left only one book. *The Conversion of the Magdalen* (1588), written to give 'the vulgar' a 'taste for holy things,'[1] was immensely popular, and mysticism is latent in its theme: 'she loved much.' 'Let us love the Lord with all our hearts, with all our strength . . . with all our powers . . . so that we may be changed into Him wholly.'[2]

The most famous of this Augustinian group is the Salamancan professor, Luis de León. Here is a writer of the first rank—perhaps the greatest of Spain's poets and cer-

[1] STUDIES, Vol. II, p. 270.
[2] OP. CIT., p. 277.

tainly one of her leading prose-writers, who devotes powers which would have given his treatment of any theme distinction to the supreme theme of the soul's quest for God. Not that that quest was by any means his only preoccupation. In his poems especially (e.g., 'The Life removed,' with its somewhat Epicurean conclusion), he is primarily a Horatian, extolling moderation and comfort, or a lover of Nature ('Night serene') or of music ('To Francisco Salinas'). His *Perfect Wife*, an essay written in magnificently sonorous prose, describes the virtues of the ideal woman—and the faults of many women who were far from ideal. The *Exposition of the Book of Job* is the type of treatise one would expect from a Professor of Biblical Studies. The mystical ideas of Luis de León are latent in a few of his poems, such as 'At the Ascension' and 'The Heavenly Life'; and are expanded more fully and clearly in *The Names of Christ* (1583-5), which has marked resemblances with Orozco's work of similar title. Though primarily expository, *The Names of Christ* has much to say of the mystical life, contains some eloquent descriptions of characteristic mystical states and occasionally looks forward to the mystic's ultimate goal:

> Thou that art Light, Love and Life, Fullness of rest, infinite Beauty, endless Wealth of Sweetness: grant Thou to me that I may be dissolved and transformed wholly into Thyself. (1)

Approximately contemporary with Luis de León are Spain's two greatest mystics, who are also two of the greatest in the whole of Christian history, the Discalced Carmelites, St. Teresa of Jesus and St. John of the Cross.

Like García de Cisneros and St. Peter of Alcántara, they were religious reformers. St. Teresa, after living for a quarter of a century in undistinguished seclusion in a convent at Ávila, conceived the idea of bringing the Carmelite Order back to the austerity of its Primitive Rule and devoted the last twenty years of her life to founding first one reformed convent at Ávila, and then, in various parts

---

(1) STUDIES, Vol. I, p. 338.

of the country, sixteen more, and indirectly, too, to develop-
ing the same reform among men, with such success that,
by the time of her death, the Discalced friars, one of the
first two of whom was St. John of the Cross, had founded
fourteen houses, and were well on the way to securing the
establishment of the Reform as a separate Order.

Yet, despite the constant travelling, the incessant letter-
writing and the gnawing financial worries involved in the
making of these foundations, to say nothing of the determined opposition which they were apt to arouse in high
places, despite growing ill-health, too, and the persecution
of the Reform by the friars of the Observance which was
at its height in the very year when she was writing with
the intensest concentration, St. Teresa, in her later years,
produced a series of works on the mystical life which
brings her, in this respect, far above the level of any other
writer yet mentioned. The *Life*, written under obedience,
and for private circulation (1562-5), is a predominantly
spiritual autobiography which traces its author's gradual
growth in mental prayer, but which one single passage—
and a digression at that: the Similitude of the Waters—
would have sufficed to make famous. The *Way of perfec-
-tion* (1565), written for the edification of the nuns in the
reformed convents, is the most easily comprehensible of
St. Teresa's works to the general reader, and only a few
chapters and passages in it can be called definitely mystical
—most of them belonging to the sensitive and highly
spiritual exposition of the Paternoster which comprises the
last sixteen chapters. Her master-work is the wholly mystical *Interior Castle* (1577), in which the contemplative's ad-
vance from Purgation to Union is pictured as a progress
from the circumference to the centre of a circular building,
through seven sets of apartments, or 'mansions', 'in the
centre and midst of which is the chiefest mansion, where
the most secret things pass between God and the soul.'[1]

---

[1] INTERIOR CASTLE, I, i (COMPLETE WORKS OF ST. TERESA OF JESUS,
London, 1946, Vol. II, p. 202).

Based almost entirely on her own experiences, St. Teresa's narrative, completely devoid of erudition, is perhaps the most remarkable document of its particular kind in existence: it is almost incredible that it should have been written amid thronging duties and harassing persecutions, and not by a skilled and learned director of souls, but by a woman. Of St. Teresa's minor works, the *Foundations* (1573-6) and the *Letters*, though of great interest, belong to the active life, but the *Spiritual Relations* (1560-81) are, like parts of the *Life*, concerned with her sublimest spiritual experiences, the *Poems*, though from any literary criterion almost negligible, are tinged with the mystical spirit and the *Conceptions of the Love of God* (c. 1571-3) and *Exclamations of the Soul to God* (? 1569) breathe the very atmosphere in which the mystic lives.

St. John of the Cross challenges Luis de León for the title of Spain's greatest poet and most critics would unhesitatingly describe him as the greatest mystic Christendom has known since the Renaissance. He is at once the poets' poet and the mystics' mystic. The three lyrics on which his literary fame rests are 'Dark Night' and 'Spiritual Canticle', which, with the most exquisite imagery and amazing technical skill, describe the soul's quest of her Beloved, and 'Living Flame of Love', which dwells on the glories of the Life of Union. On these three poems, at various dates between 1582 and 1588, their author wrote four commentaries: those on 'Dark Night' are *The Ascent of Mount Carmel* and its sequel, *Dark Night of the soul;* the other two bear the same titles as the poems on which they are written. *Living Flame of Love* is a more remarkable example of white-hot intensity of production even than the *Interior Castle*. That, it is true, is considerably the longer of the two, and the six months during which it was written were months, as we have said, of administrative preoccupations and constant apprehensions—it was not even all composed in the same place. But what other mystic could have written, in fifteen days, a book of the length of the *Living Flame of Love*, and relating 'to things so interior

and spiritual that words commonly fail to describe
them'? [1]

> O living flame of love
> That, burning, dost assail
> My inmost soul with tenderness untold,
> Since thou dost freely move,
> Deign to consume the veil
> Which sunders this sweet converse that we hold.
>
> . . . .
>
> How tender is the love
> Thou wak'nest in my breast
> When thou, alone and secretly, art there!
> Whispering of things above,
> Most glorious and most blest,
> How delicate the love thou mak'st me bear! [2]

Sublime as the book is, its author warns us that 'all which
is said herein is as far removed from all that there is to say
as is a picture from a living person.'[3] Yet here, perhaps
more than anywhere else, he has succeeded in opening a
chink of the window into the mystic's heaven-on-earth,
through which we can gain some faint idea of its nature.

When St. John of the Cross died, in the same year as
Luis de León (1591) and nine years after the death of St.
Teresa, he left behind him a school which before long grew
to such an extent that in this brief survey to make even a
roll-call of its members would be impossible. Its two most
distinguished members were Jerónimo Gracián (1545-
1614), who has already been referred to, and Tomás de
Jesús (c. 1564-1627), famous in Carmelite history as the
founder of a type of priory for solitaries known as the
Desierto. Gracián was in the main an original writer
(though his *Mystical Theology*[4] was a compendium of the
teaching of St. Bonaventura), but the chief aim of Tomás
de Jesús' works was to 'reduce to a brief summary all the
doctrine that the holy mother Teresa of Jesus wrote . . .

---

[1] COMPLETE WORKS OF ST. JOHN OF THE CROSS, Vol. III, London,
1935, p. 15.
[2] POEMS OF ST. JOHN OF THE CROSS, London, 1947, pp. 20-3.
[3] COMPLETE WORKS OF ST. JOHN OF THE CROSS, Vol. III, London, 1935,
p. 16.
[4] P. 19, above.

in the matter of prayer and things of the spirit.'[1] Such a
systematization was the *Summary and Compendium of the
Degrees of Prayer* (1610), with which was published a short
Treatise of Mental Prayer, based on other great exponents
of mystical theology. More original are the *Practice of living faith* (1613) and *Rules for examining and discerning a
soul's interior progress* (1620). Two Latin treatises, *De
Contemplatione divina* (1620) and *Divinae orationis metho-
dus*, etc. (1623), go at length into the nature of contemplation: the long controversy which has raged around the
subject of 'acquired contemplation' is believed by some to
have had its rise in the use of this phrase by Tomás de
Jesús. Among other early leading *teresianos* and *sanjuanis-
tas* are Juan de Jesús María (Aravalles), whose *Treatise on
Prayer* (1587) saw the light only in the twentieth century;
Antonio de la Cruz, who in a still unpublished *Book of
Contemplation* (c. 1595) tries to define the act of contemplation more exactly than had previously been done, even
by St. John of the Cross; Inocencio de San Andrés, author
of a *Mystical Theology and Mirror of Eternal Life* (1595),
which also glosses St. John of the Cross; and a second
Juan de Jesús María, generally referred to as 'the Calahor-
ran', who became General of his Order, and whose two
works, *Mystical Theology* and *School of prayer and contemplation*, show some divergences from the teaching of
the Carmelite Saints.

Farther than this into the long history of the Carmelite
School we cannot go, nor can we describe the later members of the Franciscan and Augustinian groups, nor those
who, belonging to other Orders, or to no Order, wrote on
mystical theology during the late sixteenth and seventeenth
centuries. Though these individuals, however, are not of
sufficient distinction to be referred to at length, mention
should be made of two significant tendencies in the later
development of Spanish mysticism within this period which
many of them illustrate.

The first is the tendency, which we have observed in

---

[1] STUDIES, Vol. II, p. 289.

Tomás de Jesús, to systematize and codify the works of others, rather than to write from one's own experience. It will be found in many other Carmelites, who confine themselves mainly to glossing the works of St. Teresa and St. John of the Cross, and also in a group of Jesuits who go beyond these two saints, and indeed beyond their Spanish contemporaries and predecessors altogether, and codify the mystical teaching of the Bible, the Fathers and certain mediæval authorities. This distinguished Jesuit group includes Juan Eusebio Nieremberg, the author of a striking treatise *On the Beauty of God* (1641); Baltasar Álvarez, one of St. Teresa's earliest and most efficient directors; Francisco de Ribera, her contemporary biographer; and Luis de la Puente, whose *Spiritual Guide* (1609), written for those who are 'walking fervently in the three ways which are called purgative, illuminative and unitive,'[1] is perhaps the earliest work in Spanish which can be called in the modern sense a treatise on mystical theology.

Secondly, there is the tendency which perverted the doctrine of the Prayer of Quiet, found in Laredo and Osuna, and developed by St. Teresa, into the false doctrine of Quietism. The first stage in this transformation can be seen in the Mercedarian Juan Falconi (1596-1638), who before his death published only one book (*A Primer whereby we may learn to read in Christ the book of eternal life*: 1637) and was so far from being thought unorthodox that a process (which proved unsuccessful) was set on foot to secure his beatification. The *Primer* makes a vigorous frontal attack upon that manifestation of pseudo-mysticism, allied to Quietism, and particularly rife at this time, known as Illuminism. Two opuscules, however, entitled *Letter written to a spiritual daughter, wherein the writer teaches her the purest and most perfect spirit of prayer*, and *Letter to a religious in defence of the manner of prayer in pure faith taught by the writer*, dated respectively 1628 and 1629, but apparently published only in Italian versions (1673 and 1674), were subsequently placed on the Index, to which,

---

[1] STUDIES, Vol. II, p. 318.

no doubt from motives of caution, was soon added the *Primer*. It would be going beyond the scope of this essay to discuss to what extent these opuscules, together with a longer work, published still later, *A Straight Road to Heaven*, may be termed quietistic, or to show how Molinos, basing himself, not merely on Falconi, but on St. Teresa, and sometimes on the Fathers, debases true mysticism by turning means into a goal. For already, before 1675, the date of the first edition of Molinos' *Spiritual Guide*, the long Golden Age of Spanish mysticism was over.

II

Two questions spring to the mind of anyone who studies this remarkable period of mystical activity, of the intensity and productiveness of which the foregoing pages have been able to give only some slight indication.

How, first of all, do we account for this unparalleled intensity of wealth of production beginning so suddenly and continuing for about a century and three quarters? And why, in the second place, has practically no mystical work, of an original kind, been produced in Spain since?

The intensity is not difficult to account for: indeed, we have an almost exact parallel in the history of the drama in Spain, which existed only in the most rudimentary form during the Middle Ages, but leapt into life with the Renaissance, became rapidly mature, produced three or four first-rank writers, and, for almost exactly the same period of time as that now under consideration, showed a fertility unsurpassed anywhere in the world. Spain has always possessed immense reserves of power, and her history has often been made by great bursts of energy manifested by individuals. It was thus that, in less than half a century, she acquired her vast empire in the Indies; and it is not surprising that she should have been equally successful in her explorations of what Juan de los Ángeles once aptly termed 'God's Indies.' Furthermore, we have to take into account the strong emotions engendered in Spain

27

by the Reformation and the Counter-Reformation, as well as the high degree of intensity which in Spanish religious experience is quite normal.

The long duration of the period during which mysticism flourished in Spain is explicable by the strong impetus given to it, at a point which might otherwise have been the beginning of a rapid decline, by the Carmelite Saints. The slow pace of the decline is attributable mainly to the persistence of the Carmelite School, which also worked indirectly through other Orders, and to the interest created and maintained by those who, though not mystics themselves, had a gift for systematizing and codifying the mystics' works. Finally, it must not be forgotten that, while a great wealth of mystical experience may be engendered in an age with little power of expression, it happened providentially that in the sixteenth and seventeenth centuries not only the energy and ardour of the contemplative, but the brilliance and the force of the Spanish language, were at their height.

The lateness and suddenness of the beginning, as has already been hinted, may be connected with, and perhaps even attributed to, the completion of the Reconquest in 1492. To have achieved freedom after nearly eight hundred years of total or partial occupation by an enemy of alien faith is an experience that has been the lot of few, if any, nations in the world's history. It was natural that for some decades the country should be in a state of extreme exaltation, and, as the Reconquest, at any rate for long periods at a time, had assumed the character of a crusade, there was no field in which that exaltation would have been expected to express itself more actively than in that of religion.

The second question is the difficult one to answer: why, after touching such great heights and exercising so wide and profound an influence, should Spanish mysticism have almost completely disappeared? Allowing a century—the rationalistic and prosaic eighteenth century, as it happens —for a reaction natural after an intensity of output un-

paralleled anywhere in post-Renaissance Europe, one would
surely expect after that to find some counter-reaction—
some appreciation of the mystics of the Golden Age if not
some fresh original manifestation of the same spirit—
during the nineteenth. But no! Religion makes frequent
appearances in nineteenth-century literature, but at best
it is an intransigent and florid institutionalism, and at worst
a picturesque and sometimes sentimental religiosity. There
is no trace of, and no interest in, the robust experiential
idealism of the Carmelite Saints. 'Many,' wrote Pidal in his
essay on Malón de Chaide (1840), 'smile derisively at the
mention of the title of a mystical work or the name of a
religious writer.'[1] Even as literature, the writings of the
greatest mystics were not appreciated. St. John of the Cross,
in his prose, said an anonymous nineteenth-century editor
of his, was inferior, not only to St. Teresa, but even to
Luis de Granada:

> He is languid, incorrect, careless in phraseology; his apostrophes
> are frequent and monotonous; his periods unequal; his com-
> binations of words inharmonious. [2]

Indeed, declares the prologist, though superior to the writers
named in the 'energy and vivacity of his sentiment', he
is inferior to them in 'intellectual capacity.'[2]

No one would get a hearing for such sentiments to-day;
yet, though appreciation of the mystics has certainly reached
a high level in Spain, the twentieth century cannot be said
to have produced any mystical literature worthy of mention.
The reason for this is of necessity a somewhat complicated
one, since the Golden Age of Spanish mysticism was the
product of so many factors—historical, religious, social,
and literary. One can perhaps best explain it by recapitu-
lating them.

First, the ground had been well prepared for some fresh
manifestation of religious activity by the successful termina-

---

[1] The essay can be conveniently read in ESTUDIOS LITERARIOS, Vol. II,
Madrid, 1890, p. 169.
[2] BIBLIOTECA DE AUTORES ESPAÑOLES, Vol. XXVII, p. xix.

tion of a crusade centuries old, and the mood of national exaltation which followed it.

Next, reform was in the air; austerity was once more welcomed; the Tridentine decrees were stiffening religious observance; new Orders were being founded, and others, which had become relaxed, were recovering their primitive strictness. All this was a call to religious people the nation over to return to mortification, recollection, and spiritual detachment, and these are precisely the exercises with which the mystical life begins.

Then there is the element of genius which acted as the spark applied to material ready for ignition. The genius was St. Teresa. 'Soul of fire,' as Antonio Machado calls her, she wrote of the mystical quest with such white-hot zeal, and yet in language so easily understood, that to hundreds of Discalced friars and nuns—and who can say to how many others?—it became something real, which they too must pursue. Not only, then, did she rescue a few writers, notably Laredo and Osuna, from the complete oblivion into which they could hardly have avoided falling, but one may be sure that she inspired numbers of the Discalced Carmelites who were to follow her, and who, without her, might never have written at all. Even writers as eminent as Luis de Granada and St. Peter of Alcántara would hardly have been read as widely as they were, or have had so much influence outside their own Orders, had not St. Teresa commended them, quoted them, used them, and swept them, as it were, into the great mystical current. She fused diverse temperaments; absorbed, reconciled, and re-expressed apparently divergent ideals. Were it not for the clearly marked differences in thought which persist in certain of the religious Orders, she might be said to have found Spanish mysticism a movement and left it a school.

Again, the richness of the content of Spanish mysticism is due largely to the strong injection of vivid personal experience which it received, once more chiefly from Carmel: without this it would have lost much of its force

30

I

and vitality. And, at the same time, it was fortunate in being able to draw on many sources outside Spain—not only on the Scriptures and the Fathers, which were accessible to all, but on Neo-Platonism, which came into Spain with the Renaissance, and on the mediæval mystics of the Low Countries, several of whom have now been shown to have had a definite and direct influence in Spain.

Finally, there is the happy chance that this age of deep religious experience coincided with a period of supreme excellence in literary expression. The vernacular, for so long despised as base and vulgar, had emancipated itself to such an extent that not only a woman like St. Teresa, but a professor at one of the 'old' universities, like Luis de León, could write in it without fear of censure. And, once emancipated, the vernacular rose to surprising heights: the age of St. John of the Cross, it must be remembered, was also the age of Cervantes, the greatest age of Spanish prose.

Those were the chief factors that combined to create this great age of Spanish mysticism, and it is chiefly because nothing approaching a similar conjunction of conditions has occurred since that there has never been another.

III

Although mysticism has found little expression in Spain since the end of its Golden Age, one must not imagine that there is any disharmony between it and the Spanish temperament. On the contrary, no traveller who knows what mysticism means can spend many weeks in Spain without perceiving that it is inborn in the Spanish people. Beneath that inflexible, and, some might suspect, conventional, institutionalism which still flourishes in reality as in literature, many Spaniards, not only in the cloister but in the world, live what is in fact a rudimentary form of the mystical life as known to the most profound contemplatives. The atmosphere in which contemplation thrives is always there. Even so heterodox a traveller as Havelock Ellis could not fail to be struck, on entering a Spanish

31

church, with 'the ecstatic attitude of devotion which the
worshippers sometimes fall into without thought of any
observer.'[1] And why should they not? They are but
following the maxim of St. John of the Cross: 'Live in this
world as though there were in it but God and thy soul, so
that thy heart may be detained by naught that is human.'[2]
And closer acquaintance with individual Spaniards will
show that much more than the atmosphere is there, and
that life and character are permeated with the recollected-
ness, the tranquillity, the singleness of purpose, and the
passionate devotion of the mystic. The iron demands made
upon the lovers of God by St. John of the Cross, which,
viewed against a mundane background, seem so terrifyingly
inhuman, are matters of stern but perfectly practicable self-
discipline to the descendants of the men who kept the flame
of crusading idealism alight, even though it flickered at
times, for eight long centuries.

So Ángel Ganivet, one of the Spaniards who has best
understood his countrymen, is right when he declares that
mysticism is the 'true centre' of the Spanish conception of
Christianity, 'so deeply rooted in Spain that we cannot take
a step in life without having it as our companion.'[3] 'Castile
is a race of mystics,' says another Spaniard, contemporary
with him. 'We have been mystics to the marrow. . . . Our
race has certainly been inoculated with mysticism.' There
may be an incapacity, he allows, for mystical expression,
but there is none for the mystical quest.[4]

Though one of the most remarkable characteristics of
that experience is the close similarity between its manifesta-
tions in different epochs, countries, and individuals, one
might expect that in a people in whom it is so firmly im-
planted, mysticism would show some strongly marked traits

---

[1] THE SOUL OF SPAIN, London, 1908, p. 13.
[2] COMPLETE WORKS OF ST. JOHN OF THE CROSS, Vol. III, London,
1935, p. 256.
[3] GRANADA LA BELLA. In OBRAS COMPLETAS, Madrid, 1943, Vol. I,
pp. 38-9.
[4] A. González Blanco: LAS MEJORES POESÍAS MÍSTICAS EN LENGUA
CASTELLANA, Madrid, 1916, pp. v, xix, xx.

of its own. The student soon discovers that this is so, though also that no one of these is characteristic exclusively of Spanish mysticism: it is the combination of them all that gives the Spanish Golden Age its individuality.

First, Spanish mysticism has little to do with philosophy. The Spaniard has always tended to turn from abstractions, subtleties, and even systems, to the concrete and substantial. He prefers action to speculation. 'It is a mystery of our race, this dislike of the abstract,' says Menéndez y Pelayo. 'The propensities of the Spanish people are all for action.'[1] 'The soul of Spain,' declares Ángel Ganivet, 'speaks through its deeds, for thoughts can be expressed in many ways, and the best way is not always by speech.' So he draws a picture of Spain leaving subtleties to the schoolmen and expressing truth in the language of war. Her 'theological and philosophical *Summa,*' he ends, 'is to be found in (the collection of national ballads known as) the *Romancero.*'[2]

This aversion to abstractions is nowhere better reflected than in the Spanish mystics. Many of them are skilled practical psychologists, superb directors of individual souls, and well able to express their experiences in works of which the appeal is not only to the few. The greatest of them owe little to their predecessors, other than the Bible and the Fathers. Even when outwardly objective, their doctrine is permeated by their own experiences. Their lives are simple, their faith is spontaneous, their conception of the 'infused science' is devoid of subtleties, and they are somewhat shy even of generalization.

Spanish mysticism is a remarkable combination of idealism and realism. Most true mystics (though not everybody is aware of the fact) are realists; for mysticism, far from being the vague, ethereal thing of popular belief, is the most exact science in existence. Its goal is as clearly envisaged as are the means which must be employed in order to reach it. Now there is the same combination of idealism and

(1) CIENCIA ESPAÑOLA, Madrid, 1887-8, Vol. I, p. 94.
(2) IDEARIUM ESPAÑOL, Madrid, 1943, Vol. I, p. 99.

C

realism in the Spaniard's character. While retaining a firm hold on life's realities, he keeps his gaze fixed upon the object of his desire, and no considerations, either material or spiritual, will deflect his will from reaching it. The Spaniard loathes compromise; and, if his strong instinct for reality tells him that he will be ruined unless he abandons his ideals, he will quietly resign himself to accepting ruin. This is no rhetoric, but a simple statement of fact, of which, in quite recent years, illustrations can be found by the thousand.

The mysticism of Spain, then, is of the purest type: in it both idealism and realism are carried to the highest possible degree. It is also—again like the Spanish character —intensely personal and individualistic. Nothing could be less like pantheism, nothing farther from self-annihilation. What has to be annihilated in the soul, as St. John of the Cross never tires of saying, is 'affections for pleasures with respect to all that is not God.' [1] A knowledge of oneself is an indispensable preliminary to a knowledge of God. The contemplative life is dominated by these two realities. It is 'Thou and I', the Lover and the Beloved, God and the soul:

> They said to the Lover: 'Whither goest thou?' He answered: 'I come from my Beloved.' 'Whence comest thou?' 'I go to my Beloved. . . .'
>
> Said the Lover to his Beloved: 'Thou art all, and through all, and in all, and with all. I will have Thee wholly that I may have and be myself wholly.' The Beloved answered: 'Thou canst not have Me wholly unless thou art Mine.' And the Lover said: 'Let me be wholly Thine and be Thou wholly mine.' [2]

And the sixteenth-century mystics are more emphatic even than this. 'I for God and God for me, and no world beside!' cries Juan de los Ángeles. [3] 'Naught is needful, save only God.' [4] 'He is the centre of our soul, the resting-place of

---

[1] Letter XI. In COMPLETE WORKS OF ST. JOHN OF THE CROSS, Vol. III, London, 1935, p. 279. Cf. for a fuller exposition, Vol. I, pp. 88 ff.

[2] BOOK OF THE LOVER AND THE BELOVED, London, 1946, §§ 25, 68.

[3] SPIRITUAL STRIFE (LUCHA ESPIRITUAL), I, xi.

[4] OP. CIT., I, x.

our desires and the sphere of our love.'[1] The hammer
strokes of the 'Maxims' of St. John of the Cross beat out
again and again the same message:

> Take thou no heed of the creatures if thou wilt keep the image
> of God clearly and simply in thy soul.
> Take God for thy Spouse and for a Friend with Whom thou
> walkest continually.
> Feed not thy spirit on aught beside God.
> Enter into thy bosom and labour in the presence of the Spouse,
> Who is ever present and loves thee well.[2]

Hardly less important, and in greater need of emphasis,
is the active character of Spanish mysticism. Even if an
impersonal creed were possible to men so robust—and the
one woman in the company is the most robust of them all
—their native individualism would save them from it. The
quietistic pseudo-mysticism which developed late in the
seventeenth century was quite foreign to the Spanish temperament. In Spain itself, indeed, little was heard of it:
Molinos spent the last twenty-five years of his life in Rome,
and the works of Falconi which were placed on the index
were first published in Rome and in Italian. The mysticism
of Spain's Golden Age is active, ardent, militant, as
befitted an ardent and militant race. It aims at affirming,
not at denying, the power of the human will. Its bowmen
bear the 'arrows of desire,' and press upon Heaven with no
'lazy breath,' but with a 'sharp dart of longing love.' St.
Teresa's contemplative presses on from mansion to mansion. Juan de los Ángeles describes the spiritual strife
between man and God or the storming of the gateways of
His Kingdom. The pilgrim in 'Dark Night' descends her
staircase, leaves the house at dead of night, and journeys
to her Beloved; 'I *went*. . . . Safe *sped* I. . . . On I
prest': all is action. The traveller, stage by stage, makes
the steep ascent of Mount Carmel, or of Mount Sion. The
betrothed cries: 'Whither hast vanishèd?' but hardly has
the cry escaped her than she speaks again in a very different
tone:

(1) OP. CIT., Proemio.
(2) 'Spiritual Sentences and Maxims.' In COMPLETE WORKS OF ST. JOHN
OF THE CROSS, Vol. III, London, 1935, pp. 243, 248, 250, 251.

'I'll seek my love straightway
Over yon hills, down where yon streamlets flow.
To pluck no flowers I'll stay;
No fear of beasts I'll know;
Past mighty, men, o'er frontier-grounds I'll go.

Even Orozco and León, for all their insistence on the joys of peace, say much about the road that leads to it. 'But I will warn thee, brother,' observes Orozco, in writing of the very highest degree of contemplation, 'that he who would see the face of that most powerful Wrestler, our boundless God, must first have wrestled with himself, and be a man perfect in the active life.'[1] There is no passivity here, but rather a *caballería a lo divino*, a divine knight-errantry. The Prayer of Quiet can be of but short duration; even the Spiritual Betrothal brings but temporary rest. Only in the state of Union can true rest be found:

All things for me that day
Ceas'd, as I slumber'd there,
Amid the lilies drowning all my care. [2]

Till that day all is energy, activity, strife.

'The tale is endless,' cries Luis de León; 'for, as I let out the sails, even then do I catch fresh vistas to be explored; and the farther I journey, the wider are the seas which come into my view.'[3] And so it will ever be with this glorious progress till the distant seas shall merge in the portless and shoreless ocean, where the work of the Lover's fulfilment shall begin.[4]

---

[1] P. 76, below.
[2] P. 113, below.
[3] NOMBRES DE CRISTO: *Face of God*.
[4] BOOK OF THE LOVER AND THE BELOVED, London, 1946, § 235.

36

LIST OF BOOKS

Particulars of editions and studies (mainly in English) of each of the authors represented in the text below will be found immediately beneath their names. So little has been written in English on Spanish mysticism as a whole that a few books in Spanish have also been included in the list of books on this subject which follows:—

Butler, Dom Cuthbert: *Western Mysticism*. London, Constable, 1922.

Crisógono de Jesús Sacramentado, P.: *La Escuela mística carmelitana*. Madrid, 1930.

Green, Otis H.: 'The Historical Problem of Castilian mysticism.' In *Hispanic Review*, 1938, Vol. VI, pp. 93-103. (Cf. also 1942, Vol. X, pp. 18-33.)

Groult, Pierre: *Les Mystiques des Pays Bas et la littérature espagnole du XVIᵉ siècle*. Louvain, 1927.

Inge, W. R.: *Christian Mysticism*. London, Methuen, 1899, pp. 213-34.

Menéndez y Pelayo, M.: *Estudios de crítica literaria*. Madrid, 1915 (3rd ed.), pp. 3-77.

Monasterio, Ignacio: *Místicos agustinos españoles*. Madrid, 1929, 2 vols.

Peers, E. Allison: *Spanish Mysticism*. London, Methuen, 1924.

Peers, E. Allison: *Studies of the Spanish Mystics*. London, Sheldon Press, 2 vols.: Vol. I, 1927 (revised and enlarged, 1951); Vol. II, 1930. All but the first of the authors excerpted are treated in these two volumes.

Peers, E. Allison: *Behind that Wall*. London, S.C.M. Press, 1947.

Rawlinson, G. C.: *An Anglo-Catholic's Thoughts on Religion*. London, Longmans, 1924, pp. 68-79.

Rousselot, Paul: *Les Mystiques espagnols*. Paris, Didier, 1867.

Sainz Rodríguez, P.: *Introducción a la historia de la literatura mística en España*. Madrid, 1927.

Underhill, Evelyn: *Mysticism*. London, Methuen, 1911 [Refers to the Spanish mystics *passim*.]

Valera, Juan: 'Del misticismo en la poesía española.' In *Discursos académicos*, Madrid, 1905, Vol. II, pp. 5-63.

EXTRACTS FROM
THE SPANISH MYSTICS

*

RAMÓN LULL

c. 1233—c. 1315

(See p. 15, above)

EDITIONS. *Blanquerna*. London, Jarrolds, n.d. [1926]. *The Book of the Lover and the Beloved*. London, S.P.C.K., 2nd ed. 1946. *The Art of Contemplation*. London, S.P.C.K., 1925. *The Tree of Love*, London, S.P.C.K., 1926. *The Book of the Beasts*. London, Burns Oates, 1927. All translated by E. Allison Peers.

STUDIES. E. Allison Peers: *Ramon Lull, a Biography*, London, S.P.C.K., 1929, and *Fool of Love*, London, S.C.M. Press, 1946. (The first is a critical, the second a·popular biography.)

A Life of Ramon Lull. Written by an unknown hand about 1311. London, Burns Oates, 1927.

A. E. Waite: *Raymond Lully*. London, Rider, 1922.

THE BOOK OF THE LOVER
AND THE BELOVED

(EXTRACTS)

The Lover asked his Beloved if there remained in Him anything still to be loved. And the Beloved answered that he had still to love that by which his own love could be increased.

Said the Lover to the Beloved: 'Thou that fillest the sun with splendour, fill my heart with love.' The Beloved answered: 'Hadst thou not fullness of love, thine eyes had not shed those tears, neither hadst thou come to this place to see Him that loves thee.'

The birds hymned the dawn, and the Lover, who is the dawn, awakened. And the birds ended their song, and the Lover died in the dawn for his Beloved.

'O bird that singest of love, ask thou of my Beloved, Who has taken me to be His servant, wherefore He tortures me with love.' The bird replied: 'If Love made thee not

41

to bear trials, wherewith couldst thou show thy love for Him?'

The Lover wept, and sang songs of his Beloved, and said: 'Swifter is love in the heart of the lover than is the splendour of the lightning to the eye, or the thunder to the ear. The tears of love gather more swiftly than the waves of the sea; and sighing is more proper to love than is whiteness to snow.'

The Lover was all alone, in the shade of a fair tree. Men passed by that place, and asked him why he was alone. And the Lover answered: 'I am alone, now that I have seen you and heard you; until now, I was in the company of my Beloved.'

The Beloved revealed Himself to His Lover, clothed in new and scarlet robes. He stretched out His Arms to embrace him; He inclined His Head to kiss him; and He remained on high that he might ever seek Him.

They asked the Lover what sign his Beloved bore upon His banner. He answered: 'The sign of a Man that was dead.' They asked him why He bore such a sign. He answered: 'Because He became Man and died on a Cross, and because they that glory in being His lovers must follow in His steps.'

Love shone through the cloud which had come between the Lover and the Beloved, and made it to be as bright and resplendent as is the moon by night, as the day-star at dawn, as the sun at midday, and as the understanding in the will; and through that bright cloud the Lover and the Beloved held converse.

Said the Lover: 'O ye that love, if ye will have fire, come light your lanterns at my heart; if water, come to my eyes, whence flow the tears in streams; if thoughts of love, come gather them from my meditations.'

'Say, O Fool! what is solitude?' He answered: 'It is solace and companionship between Lover and Beloved.'

42

'And what are solace and companionship?' 'Solitude in
the heart of the Lover,' he replied, 'when he remembers
naught save only his Beloved.'

BOOK OF THE LOVER AND THE BELOVED, §§ 1, 6, 26, 35, 38, 47, 91,
101, 123, 173, 246.

THE ART OF CONTEMPLATION
(EXTRACT)

'Divine Goodness,' said Blanquerna, 'Thou that art of
infinite greatness in eternity, Thou art the Good whence
springs all good beside; from Thy great Good comes all
that is good both great and small, and from Thy Eternity
comes all that abides. Wherefore in all wherein Thou art
Goodness and Greatness, and Eternity, I adore Thee, call
upon Thee, and love Thee above all that I can understand
and remember. And I pray Thee to make great and abiding
that good which Thou hast granted me, that I may praise
and serve Thee with all that pertains to Thy honour.'

'Eternal Greatness in power! Far greater art Thou than
I can remember or comprehend or love. My power rises
to Thee, that Thou mayest make it great and abiding, that
I may remember, comprehend and love Thy power, which
is infinite and eternal, from whose influence we trust there
may fall upon us grace and blessing, whence we ourselves
may become great and may abide even unto eternity.'

'Eternity, Thou that hast power of knowledge without
end or beginning! Thou hast given me a beginning and
created me that I may abide without end. Thou hast power
to save or to damn me. That which Thou wilt do with me
and with others Thy knowledge eternally knows and Thy
power can accomplish. For in Thy eternity is no movement or change. No power have I to know how Thou wilt
judge me, for my power and knowledge have a beginning.
So, then, may it please Thee that, whatsoever Thou wilt
do with me, my power and knowledge and abidingness in
this world may be to Thy glory and to the praise of Thine
honour.'

'Power, that hast all knowledge and will in thyself!
Knowledge, that hast all power and will in thyself! Will,
that hast all power and knowledge in thyself! Take all
my knowledge and power—for already hast Thou taken
all my will—that they may love and serve Thee. Thou, O
Power, canst know and will, inasmuch as Thou art without
increase or diminution or any change soever. Thou, O
Knowledge, dost know even as Thou dost will. And Thou,
O Will, dost will even as Thou dost will in will, power and
knowledge. Wherefore, since thus it is, and naught can
make it otherwise or different, may grace come to my
power from this great influence, that I may ever have
power, knowledge and will to honour Thy power—to my
knowledge that I may honour Thy knowledge—and to my
will that I may honour Thy love.'

'Wisdom Divine! In Thee are virtue and love. Thou
knowest Thyself to be love above all other love, and virtue
above all other virtue: Thou knowest Thyself to be Wisdom
greater than all wisdom beside. Wherefore if my knowledge perceive that my will has small virtue in loving Thy
will, Thy knowledge must needs know that Thy love is
greater in loving me than is my love in loving Thee. And
if Thou knewest not this, Thy knowledge could not know
how much greater virtue there is in Thy love and Thy will
than in mine, nor could my knowledge and will have the
virtue wherewith to contemplate God in perfection.' While
Blanquerna pursued this contemplation he bethought himself that, if God knew that His Will loved sin, He would
have no virtue wherewith to love Himself. And thus Blanquerna comprehended that, if he ceased to love God, he
would have no virtue wherewith he might cease to love sin.
So Blanquerna wept abundantly, when he remembered his
sin and guilt at such times as he had sinned.

'Love Divine! Thy Virtue is more real than that of any
love beside, and Thy Truth is more real than all truth
beside. For if the virtue of the sun can be real in giving
light, and the virtue of fire in giving warmth, far more real
is Thy Virtue in loving. For between the sun and its

splendour there is a difference, and between fire and its heat. But between Thy Love and Virtue and Truth there is no essential difference; and all that Thy Love disposes in truth, It does with infinite virtue in love and in truth; whereas all that is done by things beside is done with virtue finite in quantity and time. Wherefore, since this is so, to Thee, O Love, O Virtue, O Truth, I bind and submit myself all the days of my life, that I may honour Thy graces, and proclaim to unbelievers, and to Christians who have lost their devotion, the truth of Thy Virtue and Thy Truth and Thy Love.'

Virtue, Truth and Glory met in the thoughts of Blanquerna, when he contemplated his Beloved. Blanquerna considered to which of these three he would give the greatest honour in his thoughts and will; but since he could conceive in them no difference soever, he gave them equal honour in remembering, comprehending and desiring his Beloved. And he said: 'I adore Thee, O Virtue, that hast created me; I adore Thee, O Truth, that shalt judge me; I adore Thee, O Glory, wherein I hope to be glorified in Virtue and Truth, which will never cease to give glory without end.'

Blanquerna enquired of the Truth of his Beloved: 'If in Thee Glory and Perfection were not that which Thou art, what then wouldst Thou be?' And Understanding answered Blanquerna: 'What but falsehood, or a truth like to that of thine, or naught at all, or that in which there would be affliction everlasting?' And Blanquerna said: 'And if Truth were not, what then would Glory be?' And Memory answered: 'It would be naught.' 'And if Perfection were not, what would Glory be?' 'It would be that which is naught, or nothingness.'

THE ART OF CONTEMPLATION, Chapter II.

GARCÍA DE CISNEROS
1455—1510
(See p. 16 above)

EDITIONS. *Book of Exercises for the Spiritual Life.* Trans. E. Allison Peers. Montserrat, 1929.

STUDIES. E. Allison Peers: 'The Dawn of the Golden Age: García de Cisneros.' In *Studies of the Spanish Mystics,* London, Sheldon Press, Vol. II, 1930, pp. 1-37, 401-5.

HOW OUR THOUGHT IS LIFTED UP TO GOD THROUGH QUICK AND FERVENT LOVE

We have described above how the understanding is lifted up to God by meditation upon His perfections and praises, and how through the prayer of words and that of enkindled desires it becomes enkindled in love of Him. We shall now describe how the spirit, which for some time has been exercised in the manner aforesaid, is lifted up to God without any labour of the understanding or of aught else soever, and is united with Him, the which union is called by the saints true wisdom. As St. Dionysius says, this wisdom is known as ignorance; for no kind of reasoning or understanding or human knowledge can raise the exercitant to a union after this manner, such union and such feelings being the work of God alone, Who wills to give Himself to such a spirit as this without labour of understanding on its part, but Himself aiding the affections. Wherefore it seems that our soul at this stage is receptive rather than active with regard to the understanding, and that the affection of love alone reigns within it, and neither sense nor understanding has any part therein. This is the wisdom whereof St. James says that every perfect gift

46

descends from above—that is to say, from God. This wisdom is likewise that which is so greatly exalted in the Book of Wisdom. It is not, like knowledge of other kinds, born within us, being begotten by the understanding, but it arises from the exercising of our inward affections, whereof the prophet David speaks, saying: *Renuit consolari anima mea: memor fui Dei et delectatus sum et defecit spiritus meus.* That is to say that the soul which has cast away all human and fleshly delight, and is touched by this Divine wisdom, is made to rejoice by the touch of God, and lifted up on high, so that it faints away; for it suffices not to declare after any manner that which here it feels concerning its most sovereign and beloved Lord.

This wisdom has never been understood by philosophers, nor by any such as fix their understanding on bodily or fantastic objects. It is greater than all the gifts that are infused within us, with respect to the manner wherein the loftiest part of the soul is raised to God, through love; for it finds no rest in aught that is lower than God, nor yet in God himself in that which concerns its own delight or profit, but only in the love of Him Who alone is supremely to be loved. Him it seeks and desires and loves because it feels Him to be the supreme good, and not alone supreme in goodness, but likewise far withdrawn from all defect and misery.

The blessed St. Dionysius says in the seventh Book of his *De Divinis Nominibus* that this wisdom attains to God, its Beloved, through love, that it wearies not itself in speculations concerning Him, or in thinking of Him in any lofty speculative way whatsoever, unless this awakens love; as, for example, speculation upon the Holy Trinity, the generation of the Son, or the creation of the world, in all of which things the power of God is displayed, but there is no incitement therein to love. The soul is moved to love only by such meditations as raise it on high and enkindle it in love for its Creator and Lord, being conscious of Him without corporal similitudes whatsoever, and understanding Him after a manner that cannot be explained, so that, against

47

the usual course of nature, He is loved before He is known. And the manner wherein He is loved and known can be felt, but no tongue can describe it, for all this is the work of pure spirit, and naught that is corporal aids it. For our Lord God works here through Himself alone, and in this manner any person, however simple, whether a peasant or a simple old woman, may through this lofty wisdom be quickly changed into a learned disciple, if it please God to give him thereof in great quantity or in small. And this last will depend upon the preparation which a man has made, for, if he prepares not himself, nor does that which in him lies, he will never attain to this manner of wisdom.

BOOK OF EXERCISES FOR THE SPIRITUAL LIFE, Chapter XXVIII.

BERNARDINO DE LAREDO
1482—1540
(See p. 18, above)

EDITIONS. The only modern edition of the *Ascent of Mount Sion* is in Spanish: *Místicos franciscanos españoles*, Madrid, Biblioteca de Autores Cristianos, Vol. II, 1948, pp. 13-442.

STUDIES. P. Fidèle de Ros: *Le Frère Bernardin de Laredo*. Paris, J. Vrin, 1948. (The only full-length study.) E. Allison Peers: 'An exponent of "Quiet": Bernardino de Laredo.' In *Studies of the Spanish Mystics*, London, Sheldon Press, Vol. II, 1930, pp. 39-76, 406-7.

HOW THE PRACTICE OF QUIET TEACHES THE SOUL TO RISE ON WINGS OF LOVE

Whenever in this third book mention is made of 'infused science', or 'hidden wisdom', or 'secret or mystical theology', or the 'practice of aspiration', it is to be understood that a sudden and momentary uplifting of the mind is meant, in which the soul, by Divine instruction, is suddenly upraised so as to unite itself, through pure love, by the affective way alone, with its most loving God, without any interposition of thought, or of any working of the intellect or the understanding, or of natural reason. We said before that this operation transcends all reason and human understanding, and we can also say with absolute certainty that the mysteries of our true and spotless Catholic faith—such as the supreme mysteries of the Incarnation of the Divine Word, and of the Most Holy Sacrament of the Altar, and many others—are neither based upon natural reason nor admit of comprehension. We have, therefore, to understand that this Divine operation passes both reason and understanding, and that by it the soul is raised in a moment upon

49

D

the wings of love and is united with its God as often as it pleases the Divine condescension, without the interposition of the thought of any created thing.

Our own part in this sovereign operation is difficult in the beginning, but if we persevere in this upraising of our affective nature with all our might, we reach that degree of facility of which high contemplatives say that the well-schooled soul can rise to it in a moment, almost as often as it will, and become united with Him through love. And concerning this St. Dionysius says (and Herp and Henry of Balma, both high contemplatives, affirm it) that in the practised soul this happens as often as it pleases, and with such facility that they cannot predict it.

And it should be observed that the soul in this state of union—in this rising to its God—gives no more than its own free-will. For it is our God that works, and, as He works again and again with this free-will which is given by the soul, and with its raising of the affective nature, inspired by the love given it by God, it reaches a state of felicity—and even in these times there are certainly some whom Our Lord permits to affirm and bear witness that this is a very great truth.

It will be realized with the deepest joy that facility in this blessed upraising of the soul comes not of the soul's own solicitude and frequent practice, but of the continual visitations which it receives from its most loving God, and for which it disposes itself with purity of intention. For the oftener it is visited by its great Reviver, so much the more impeded does it feel from asking to receive this love again. So often does our Lord and loving Physician visit the soul that is faint for His love that He brings it to a point at which it cannot, and would not, escape from the arrows of love. For it is never without the Physician Who, looking at it, heals it so completely that it has but to cry out of a sudden concerning its grievous sickness and straightway it has its remedy. And this remedy is the visit of its Beloved Physician, Who heals it of love's affliction even before it is afflicted,

And concerning this it must be realized that there cannot be, nor was there ever, a king so powerful that with the
strongest force of arms and with many munitions he could
vanquish another king or lord so felicitously as the enamoured soul can vanquish, capture and hold its loving
Lord by means of love alone. And the reason for this is
as follows. As it is His clemency that vanquishes Him, and
as the conquest is followed by the combat of the loving
soul and the blows are of love, it is necessary that he who
does battle be taken captive, and that the captive take
his opponent prisoner also. And may He be ever our
protection.

ASCENT OF MOUNT SION, Part III, Chapter IX.

HOW THE SLEEP OF THE SOUL'S FACULTIES QUICKENS IT FOR THE FLIGHT OF LIVING LOVE

In the second chapter of the Book of the Canticles, [1] the
Church's Spouse, Christ Jesus our Beloved, says these melli-
fluous words : 'My dove is one only, etc.' Elsewhere He calls
her 'my dove' and begs her to open to Him. Now since,
as is explained in Chapter 17, the Church is the inheritance
of Jesus Christ, and every righteous soul is part of this
inheritance, and since our God calls this His Church a dove,
it follows that, when the soul knows Holy Church (of
which it is a part), it longs to receive, from this wondrous
dove, wings of living desire, with which wings it can rise
in loving flight to its most loving God, in Whom is its true
consolation.

And therefore said our authority, the Psalmist, in the
person of the enamoured soul, 'Who will give me the wings
of a dove?' That is to say: 'Who will implant in me

(1) Actually this passage is in Canticles VI, 8.

51

the desire and yearning of Holy Church to seek my God in perfect contemplation?' And since, while the soul continues in this mortal life, true rest is impossible to it without frequent interruption, that counsel must be realized which, in the sixty-seventh Psalm, is given by the Psalmist to all righteous souls, under the figure of Holy Mother Church, the inheritance of our God, spouse of Jesus Christ, our dove devoid of gall, which, desiring that those who are both her children and God's should have her wings, speaks to them after this wise: 'Though ye shall sleep between two landmarks, or places, or inheritances (or, as the gloss has it, in the authority of two testaments), ye shall be as a dove with wings of silver, and her wings shall be as if she is a silver dove, and the back of the dove shall be as finely polished gold.'

For that reason he says: 'Though ye should sleep, etc.' Sleep as to temporal things signifies paying little heed to them. Now from the small heed which the righteous soul pays to all that is not God proceeds spiritual sleep, in which the faculties of such souls slumber and are infused and transformed into the love of their God, in purity of substance. In such a way does this come to pass that the soul, in this manner of sleeping, in its inward quietness, receives the operation of none of its faculties, nor has its comprehension to do with any created thing, but is wholly spiritual. It is to this restful slumber, to this sleep of the soul's faculties, to this its repose, to this flight of the spirit in quiet contemplation, to this path of aspiration that the Prophet invites, and it is in order that the soul may take flight in this aspiration that he desires it to have wings. And he describes these as the wings of a dove, because the dove is a loving bird which, representing the Church, represents to us the same love in the Most Holy Spirit.

Therefore the Psalmist says: 'Though ye should sleep, etc.' From this we can see that this peaceful slumber, this blessed sleep which unites the soul with God, had been experienced by David when he said in the fourth Psalm: In the peace and tranquillity of that secret hiding-place in which God is found within the interior of the soul, 'I will both lay me down in peace and sleep' in the peace of this my Lord.

The Psalmist continues as follows: 'Between two landmarks,' or 'between two domains.' Here we must note that the soul which is skilled in quiet contemplation sleeps in this way as regards temporal things, and pays so little heed to them, because it is coming the nearer to God, that only for love of Him can it forbear to neglect these things to which it is obliged by charity and obedience and by the bare necessity of satisfying its own genuine scanty needs. Now the neglect of these transient things withdraws the soul from all that is transitory, as far as its affections are concerned, and the burning desires for eternal blessings upraise it to the world which shall endure for ever. So neglect for the present and desire for the future cause the soul to be as it were mortified, asleep and suspended midway between two domains—namely, between this present death and the life which is to come. So sleep here means suspension and quiet silence. And the two landmarks are this transient world and that world which is everlasting.

ASCENT OF MOUNT SION, Part III, Chapter XIX.

ST. IGNATIUS OF LOYOLA
1491—1556
(See p. 17, above)

E D I T I O N S. Of the numerous translations into English of the *Spiritual Exercises*, two representative examples are a Roman Catholic one, edited by Joseph Rickaby, London, 1915, and an Anglican one, edited by W. H. Longridge, London, Robert Scott, 1919.

S T U D I E S. The bibliography is very extensive: only a few studies in English are mentioned below.

J. Brodrick: *The Origin of the Jesuits*. London, Longmans, 1940.

E. Allison Peers: 'St. Ignatius of Loyola,' in (i) *Studies of the Spanish Mystics*, London, Sheldon Press, Vol. I, 1927, pp. 1-30, 414-22; (ii) *Behind that Wall*, London, S.C.M. Press, 1947, pp. 64-70.

H. D. Sedgwick: *Ignatius Loyola. An attempt at an impartial biography*. London, Macmillan, 1923.

Francis Thompson: *Saint Ignatius Loyola*. London, Burns Oates, 1909. Reprinted, Dublin, 1951.

Paul Van Dyke: *Ignatius Loyola, the founder of the Jesuits*. London, 1926.

A CONTEMPLATION TO OBTAIN LOVE

Two things should be noted first of all. The first of these is that love ought to show itself by actions more than by words. The second, that love consists in communication on either side—that is, in the lover's giving and communicating to the beloved what he has, or of what he has or can give. So that if the one has knowledge he will communicate it to the other, who has not; if honours, honours; if riches, riches; and so on.

The usual prayer.

The first preamble is a composition, which here is to see how I am in the presence of God our Lord, of the angels and of the saints who are interceding for me.

The second is to ask for what I want: in this case it will be to ask for an interior knowledge of all the blessings I have received, so that I may make a full acknowledgment of them and may thus in everything be able to love and serve His Divine Majesty.

The first point is to call to mind the benefits received—creation, redemption and individual gifts—pondering with deep affection upon all that Our Lord has done for me, and all that He has given me of what He has, and how, consequently, the same Lord desires to give Himself to me in so far as He can, according to His Divine ordinance. Then I shall reflect upon myself and consider what, with great reason and justice, I can for my own part offer and give to His Divine Majesty—namely, all I have, and myself with it, as one who makes an offering, with deep affection: 'Take, Lord, and receive all my freedom, my memory, my understanding, and all my will, all that I have and possess. Thou gavest it to me; to Thee, Lord, I return it. All is Thine; dispose of it wholly according to Thy will. Give me Thy love and grace: they are sufficient for me.'

The second point is to consider how God dwells in the creatures and in the elements, giving them being; in the plants, giving them growth; in the animals, giving them feeling; in man, giving him understanding; and so in me, giving me being, life, feeling and understanding; and likewise making a temple of me, since I am created in the similitude and image of His Divine Majesty. Then I should spend a similar length of time reflecting upon myself in the way described under the first head, or in any other way that I think better. The same practice should be followed in respect of each of the points which follow.

The third point is to consider how God works and labours for my sake as regards all created things on the face of the earth—*id est, habet se ad modum laborantis*, as in the heavens, elements, plants, fruits, herds, etc., giving them being, preserving them, giving them growth, feeling, etc.—and then to reflect upon myself.

The fourth point is to consider how all blessings and

gifts come down from above, just as the measure of my own power derives from the supreme and infinite Power on high; also righteousness, goodness, pity, mercy, etc., just as the rays of sunlight come down from the sun, the waters proceed from the spring, etc. After this, to reflect upon myself, as has been described, and to end with a colloquy and a *Pater noster*.

SPIRITUAL EXERCISES

FRANCISCO DE OSUNA
c. 1497—c. 1541
(See p. 18, above)

E D I T I O N S. Only of the *Third Spiritual Alphabet* is there an edition in English. (Translated by a Benedictine of Stanbrook. London, Burns Oates, 1931.) Of the *Fourth Spiritual Alphabet*, or *Ley de amor santo*, an edition in Spanish has been published in the Biblioteca de Autores Cristianos (*Místicos franciscanos*, Madrid, 1948, Vol. I, pp. 215-700).

S T U D I E S. E. Allison Peers: In *Studies of the Spanish Mystics*, London, Sheldon Press, Vol. I, 1927, pp. 77-131, 430-3.

P. Fidèle de Ros: *Le Père François d'Osuna: Sa vie, son œuvre, sa doctrine spirituelle*. Paris, Beauchesne, 1937. (The only full-length study.)

OF THE NATURE OF RECOLLECTION

This art is called the art of love, which is said to be strong like death, the vanquisher of all men. From this it is to be understood that this exercise contains in itself both art and strength, which are the two best means for vanquishing all things.

It is also called union, for, when man attains to God in this way, he becomes one spirit with Him by an exchange of wills, so that the man wills only what God wills and God does not withdraw Himself from the will of the man. So in everything they are as one, like things that are perfectly united, which, as it were, are no longer themselves, but are wholly transformed into a third. It is this that happens in this business, for, if previously God and man had diverse wills, they are now in complete agreement without dissatisfaction of either. And from this it results that the man is at unity with himself and with his fellows: were we, the multitude of the faithful, all so, we should be one in soul and heart together in the Holy Spirit, the beginning of Whose procession is found in the Father and the Son. He it is Who makes us to be one in love, that He may beget us

in grace, and bring us all to be made one together with God,
that He may not have to bring us to Him singly.

This exercise is also termed profundity, which term includes both darkness and depth; for it is based upon the
deep and profound heart of man, which must indeed be
dark—that is, bereft of human understanding—so that the
Spirit of God may come upon its darkness, and the waters
of its desires, and say: 'Let there be made Divine light. . . .'

Furthermore, it is the coming of the Lord to the soul,
for by its means the Lord visits His own who call upon
Him with sighs.

And it is called a height which raises up the soul, and
friendship or the opening of the devout heart to the Heart
of Christ.

And it is called spiritual ascension with Christ, and cap-
tivity with which we subject our understanding to Him.

And it is the third heaven to which contemplatives are
caught up.

Why should I say more? This exercise is a refuge to
which we may betake ourselves when we see storms
near; it is a constant resistance to the princes of darkness,
who secretly make war on us; a restitution which we make
to God in rendering Him all that of Himself is in us without making any reservation. It is a resurrection to spiritual
life, wherein the righteous man is given all power in Heaven
over his soul and in earth over his body; it is a continuous
attitude of reverence which we have toward God, when we
are hushed before Him in fear; it is a tree of virtues
blossoming like roses; it is the kingdom of God which we
must gain by conquest and by art, since we have it within
us and we pray for it every day; it is a royal priesthood,
by which, when we are masters of ourselves, we may offer
ourselves to God; it is a silence made in the Heaven of our
souls, though a brief one and not as lasting as the righteous
man wishes; it is a service which we render only to God,
adoring His Majesty alone; it is a seat which we have made
ready for Him that He may abide in our innermost house;
it is a tent for the wanderer in the desert; it is our most

strong tower of refuge from which we may keep watch on heavenly things; a golden vessel in which we lay up manna in the ark of our inmost being; a valley in which abounds the richest and fullest wheat; a victory which overcomes our lesser world, and subjects it wholly to God; a vineyard to be tended with vigilance and the shade that we greatly long for, where we taste of its fruit; it is the unction from the Holy Spirit, which teaches all things; it is a garden enclosed on all sides, the key of which is given to God alone, that He may enter whensoever He will.

THIRD SPIRITUAL ALPHABET, Part VI, Chapters II, III.

OF THREE WAYS OF PRAYER

The first form or manner of prayer is vocal, according to which we say that they who recite the Divine office pray, as also do they that say any prayers whatsoever, pronouncing them with the lips in praise of the Lord. Among these the most blessed prayer of the 'Pater noster' takes the first place. . . . He who says this prayer with devotion prays to the Father in the Name of the Son Who made it and therefore he is the more quickly heard of Him; so much the more quickly than they who say other prayers as the Author of this was dearer than the authors of other such to the Eternal Father.

The Lord commanded us that when we prayed we should not be given to much speaking, but multiply affection and love rather than words: a precept which the Lord Himself kept in this prayer, which is short and begins with the words 'Our Father'. Of these, the first awakens love for God, since we call Him Father, and the second love for our neighbour, since the word 'Our' makes him our brother, and a son of God by grace: we pray for him as well as for ourselves when we call the Lord Universal Father of all men. At the end of all other prayers the Church adds:

59

May this be done through our Lord Jesus Christ. But there is no need to add this in the Lord's Prayer, because by its form of address, as St. Cyprian says, the Father recognizes the words of His Son, and also because the Lord Himself was wont many times to say it when He uttered vocal prayers in His own Person or in the persons of His faithful. For these knew that prayer before any other, since the Apostles taught it to them; and of none do we read that they made any common prayer to teach others to offer save this prayer alone. . . .

Such are the excellences of this most Christian prayer that, as we find references to the Song of Songs, the Day of Days, the Holy of Holies, so we should call this the Prayer of Prayers. . . .

Although, as we have said, this Lord's Prayer has primacy over all other vocal prayers, a man should not for that reason give up the rest, lest weariness be engendered thereby. Besides, we find that some holy persons have made other approved prayers, and often, too, it is an excellent thing for a man to frame vocal prayers with words dictated by his own affection. The Scriptures are full of such prayers . . . and this manner of vocal prayer is most effectual, for it obtains of the Lord quickly that which it demands, and therefore the devout and faithful should use it much in their necessities, making these known to the Lord in few words of their own composing. Not only before they sleep, but before any task, should all pray after this manner, commending to the Lord everything in turn, speaking familiarly with Him in words prompted by their affections. In such words they may sometimes make their needs known to God, at other times confess their sins, and at others beg for mercy and grace and favour against the perils and fatigues of the world by which they or theirs are assailed.

The second manner of prayer is that within the heart, wherein the mouth pronounces no words vocally, but the heart speaks with the Lord, and we ask Him within ourselves for all that of which we have need. Then, as in a secret place, with none hearing us, we speak to the Lord, and are alone with Him; and here His favours are wont to be greater, for we speak as it were in the ear of God. In this manner prayed David, when he said to God: Thy servant hath found his heart to pray to Thee. . . .

To this manner of prayer, which the heart makes to God while the tongue is silent, may be assigned all devout and holy thoughts, whether of the Lord's Passion or of the Church, the Judgment, or any other devout thing. For it is manifest that they are praying who think and meditate upon the Sacred Passion, and even they who think upon their sins as they ought, since they think upon them only to beg mercy for them.

For this manner of prayer, which consists in holy thoughts, it is needful that a man should commit to memory the devout stories and mysteries of the Lord, and many of the good things which he hears and reads, which should be as fuel feeding the fire upon the altar of the Lord. The most fruitful thoughts, nevertheless, of all that a man may have are those of the Sacred Passion. . . . This second manner of prayer, which is the thinking and using of holy thoughts, would not seem to be fitting to beginners nor to the unlettered. Yet it is not wholly foreign to them, for they are obliged at times to think holy thoughts, since they cannot but desire happiness and many other sovereign gifts, such as to love God above all things, which they cannot do without thinking upon Him, one quality of love being to think for some time upon the Beloved. They have also obligation to receive the holy sacraments, which presupposes. some meditation and holy thoughts whereby a man prepares himself for such great gifts.

I spoke of the desire for felicity, for if we never think upon it we shall never have it; but nevertheless the religious and the recluse who have left the world to devote themselves to contemplation have obligations in this manner of prayer, and their opportunities are, or should be, far greater, by reason of the sanctuary of their Order, which is established and set apart for the perfecting of prayer. So, as vocal prayer is a thing common to devout men and women in the world, this second way of prayer should be common to all good religious in a convent, which must be a house of prayer, and not a den of thieves. This last it will be if the alms of others are spent, not in prayer, but in murmuring and wandering about, contrarily to the will of those that gave them: for this is naught but spoliation and robbery. For all those that use the things of others, but not according to the will and good intention of their owners, of a certainty usurp that which is not their own and may be called robbers; and most evidently the will of those that give such alms is that we may have opportunities of praying to the Lord without distractions. So that if we do not this we run contrary to the prime intention of the benefactor, whose debtors, as I see it, we are. Men give us their alms, indeed, for the love of God, but on condition that by means of it we serve the same Lord God better; if it were not so, they would not give it us save in case of extreme necessity, with the object of saving the lives of their neighbours.

The third manner of prayer is called mental or spiritual, whereby the highest part of our soul, in the greatest purity and affection, is raised to God upon the wings of desire and devout affection strengthened by love. The greater is this love, the fewer are the words it has, and the more comprehensive are those words and the more effective; for love, if it be true love, seeks not tedious and subtle reasonings, but works great things in silence, knowing that, if it withdraw itself from the creatures and take shelter in God, it will be unreservedly received by Him, the more so according as it is the more completely and fervently recollected.

Of those that pray thus the Lord says in the Gospel: The true worshippers shall worship the Father in spirit and in truth—for God is a Spirit and they that worship Him must worship Him in spirit and in truth—for such He seeketh to worship Him. The greater is the conformity between him who prays and the Lord to Whom he prays, the more acceptable will be the prayer; so that, as the Father is in Himself pure spirit and has nothing that is of the body, our

62

prayer will be the more welcome to Him the farther it is withdrawn from the imagination, and even from the thoughts of the heart. For these cannot be so high as not to be full low by comparison with the Lord, whereas the desires that embrace God in His Essence and without the intermediacy of bodily parts, and the love that has no care for words, these pray to God with the greatest purity and in the closest and most spiritual way, for the soul that prays thus says naught save those words in the Song of Songs: My Beloved is mine and I am His. No words could be more spiritual, more recollected or more comprehensive than these, nor could any express more of the aim of prayer to those that experience it.

That which God can do for His Lover beyond this is to give Himself to him, and that which man can do further is to give himself to God; we cannot, however, do the latter thing without His grace, and therefore said the Bride first of all: 'My Beloved is mine' rather than 'I am my Beloved's.' It is to be observed, moreover, that this self-giving of man to God, and of God to man, is a gift so perfectly given that when it is given God seems to be wholly and entirely in man. I mean that, did faith not enlighten the man who possesses God, one might almost say that within himself is comprehended the whole of God, and that apart from him He is not. At times the righteous soul sees itself so full of God that the narrowness of its bosom seems to confine His Presence, though in fact He is without limit. The gift which in the giving of themselves recollected souls offer at times to God is likewise so abundant that for themselves they keep nothing; in this way they lose their free choice and their will, and so entirely are they mindful of God and given up to Him that they are as forgetful of themselves as though they were not.

Of these three manners of prayer the Wise Man says: 'See how in three ways I have declared it to thee.' These three ways the interlineal gloss explains by saying that they are in word, which is vocal prayer, in thought, which is the prayer of the heart, and in work, which is the spiritual prayer of recollection; which, if it be real, as far exceeds the other two as work exceeds word and thought.

THIRD SPIRITUAL ALPHABET, Part XIII, Chapters I-IV, *passim.*

OF THREE WAYS OF SILENCE

There are three ways of holding one's peace in recollection, or three ways of silence, leaving aside others which are less to our point. The first is when all fantasy and imagination and forms of visible things cease in the soul, which is thus silent to all created things. The same was described by holy Job, when he said: Now should I have slept and been still, and in my sleep I should have rested with kings and counsellors of the earth, which built for themselves desolate places. We sleep to temporal things, and are silent within ourselves, as St. Gregory says, when within the secret place of our soul we withdraw into contemplation of the Creator. And the saints, who are here called kings and counsellors, build for themselves desolate places when they desire naught of this world and are oppressed in their heart by no tumult of inordinate desire, but with the right hand of holy meditation cast out from their bed, which is the heart, all unlawful impulses, despising all transitory things and immoderate cogitations which are born thereof; and, as they desire only the eternal mansions, and love naught of this, world, they enjoy great tranquillity of soul.

The second way of silence which is in recollection is that when the soul that is most still in itself enjoys a kind of spiritual ease, sitting with Mary at the feet of the Lord, and saying: I will hear what the Lord God shall say in me. To which the Lord answers: Hearken, O daughter, and consider, and incline thine ear, forget also thine own people and thy father's house.

This second way of silence may fitly be compared to the act of hearing, for the hearer is not only silent as regards all around him, but he desires all to keep silence for him, that he may turn the more completely towards Him that

64

is speaking to him, especially if, as in the present case, he
knows not where He is; for, as is said in the Gospel, we
hear the voice of God—that is, His inspiration—and we
cannot tell whence it cometh nor whither it goeth; hence
it is fitting that we should keep great silence and listen most
intently to Him. So we have two ways of silence: the one is
that wherein our imaginings cease, together with the
thoughts that revolve in our memory; the other is a for-
getting of our very selves, and a turning of the whole of
our inward man entirely toward God alone.

The first silence is when outward things no longer speak
to us; the second is of a most calm rest in which we are
silent to our very selves and dispose ourselves to God with
a submission that is receptive and prepared for Him. This
is figured by the sacred animals of Ezekiel, of which it is
said: 'And there was a voice above the firmament that was
over their heads, when they stood, and had let down their
wings.' The voice, as I said, is the Divine inspiration which
is received in the ear of the soul without sound of words
but with the presence of God only which makes itself felt;
and for this reason says Job that secretly and quietly he
heard the hidden word which was told him, and perceived,
as it were, the veins and traces of His smallest whisper.

This inspired voice is above the firmament, that is, in the
highest part of the reason, which is closely united with God
by love. The sacred winged animals are contemplatives;
and they are said to be standing, because when the voice
is heard in the soul it rises to great heights and remains
suspended, almost transported in God, as were the Apostles
when they saw Him ascend into Heaven. And so Ezekiel
was commanded to stand upon his feet that God might
speak to him: to be standing, as St. Gregory says, denotes
silent wonder, for it makes us dependent upon God, as Job
had elected that his soul should be, so that the working
of the soul's faculties all but ceases, and, as this grows less,
the soul receives wisdom.

To let down the wings signifies to put forth one's highest
powers and so to receive the Divine influence which is

poured into the soul: in which, as the gloss observes, the contemplative counts his own strength of no avail. Nevertheless, he directs it silently towards God, so that, though in himself he fails, he may find himself in Him, even as one said: 'My soul refused consolation. I thought upon God and rejoiced, I exercised myself and my spirit failed.'

The third silence of our understanding is brought to pass in God, when the soul is wholly transformed in Him and tastes abundantly of His sweetness, in which it sleeps as in a wine-cellar, and keeps silence, because it desires nothing more. For it has found satisfaction, seeing itself so far deified and united with its pattern, and clothed in the brightness of God like another Moses who has entered into the cloud which was above the mount. This was that which more truly befel St. John when after the Last Supper he leaned upon the Lord's breast, and kept silence for a space concerning all that he felt.

In this third silence it comes to pass that the understanding is so still and so entirely closed—or rather, occupied—that it understands naught of that which is said to it, nor can judge of aught that passes near it, since it neither hears nor sees. Concerning this an old man whom I confessed, who had practised these things for more than fifty years, told me, among other mysteries, that he had often listened to sermons and things of God without understanding a word of them: so hushed and so busy was his innermost understanding that nothing which was of creatures could take shape within it. I told him that he should withdraw into retirement at such times, to which he replied that voices were to him as the sound of organs, in which the soul took delight even though it understood them not: he praised the Lord as it were in a counterpoint upon them, in a way that could be felt, although he could not convey the feeling to others.

THIRD SPIRITUAL ALPHABET, Part XXI, Chapter IV.

ST. PETER OF ALCÁNTARA
1499—1562
(See p. 18, above)

E D I T I O N S. *A Golden Treatise of Mental Prayer.* Ed. G. S. Hollings. London, 1905. *Treatise of Prayer and Meditation.* Trans. Dominic Devas. London, Burns Oates, 1926.

S T U D I E S. A. O'Connor: *The Life of St. Peter of Alcántara.* Bedworth, 1915.

E. Allison Peers: 'St. Peter of Alcántara,' in *Studies of the Spanish Mystics,* London, Sheldon Press, Vol. II, 1930, pp. 97-120, and in *Behind that Wall,* London, S.C.M. Press, 1947, pp. 71-8. Much of the bibliography in *Studies,* etc. (pp. 411-16) is concerned with the disputed authorship of the *Treatise of Prayer and Meditation.*

A COUNSEL TO BE OBSERVED IN THE EXERCISE OF PRAYER AND MEDITATION

Let the last and most important counsel be that we endeavour in this holy exercise to unite meditation with contemplation, using the one as a ladder by which we may mount to the other. It must be borne in mind, then, that the function of meditation is a studious and attentive consideration of Divine things and a passing from one to another, so that the heart may be moved to a certain degree of affection and feeling for them. It is as though one should strike a flint, to draw a spark from it.

But contemplation is as though the spark had already been obtained—I mean that the affection and feeling which were sought have now been experienced, and the soul is enjoying it in repose and silence, not by much reasoning and speculation of the understanding, but by simply gazing upon the truth. Hence a holy doctor says that meditation reasons with profit and with labour, but contemplation with profit and without labour. The one seeks, the other finds; the one chews its food, the other tastes it; the one reasons and invents considerations; the other is content

67

simply to look at things for which it already has love and enjoyment. In short, the one is a means, the other an end; the one is a path and movement, the other is the end of this path and movement.

From this may be inferred a well-known precept, taught by all the masters of the spiritual life (though ill understood by those who read it): namely that, just as the means are done with when the end is reached, and as navigation is over when a boat comes into port, just so when, by means of the labour of meditation, a man attains the rest and enjoyment of contemplation, he should then have done with that holy and toilsome quest. And, content with the simple sight and thought of God—as though he had Him present —he enjoys such affection as is granted him, whether it be of love, of wonder, of joy, or aught else of the kind. The reason for giving this counsel is that, as the end of the whole matter consists rather in love and in the affections of the will than in intellectual speculation, the will being already taken and captured by this affection, we must dispense with all reasonings and intellectual speculations, in so far as we can, so that the soul, with all its strength, may occupy itself in this instead of dispersing itself through the acts of the other faculties.

Hence one doctor advises that, when a man has felt himself to be enkindled with love for God, he should at once abandon all these reasonings and thoughts, however lofty they may seem, not because they are bad, but because in that case they become impediments to some greater good, which is nothing more than cessation from movement when the goal has been reached and the abandonment of meditation for love of contemplation. This may be done, in particular, at the end of the whole exercise—that is, after the prayer for the love of God, of which we have treated above. It should be done, first of all, because it is to be presumed that, once the toil of the exercise is over, it will have produced some affection and feeling for God, since, as the wise man says, 'Better is the end of a prayer than the beginning thereof.' And secondly because, after the toil of meditation and prayer, it is but right that a man should give some small respite to his understanding, and allow it to rest in the arms of contemplation. For a man can now thrust aside all the imaginings that present themselves to him, hush the understanding, calm the memory, and fix it upon Our Lord, realizing that he is in His presence and making no speculations for the time upon the things that pertain to God.

Let him be content with the knowledge of Him that he has through faith, and apply his will and his love, since with love alone can he embrace Him and in it is the fruit of all meditation. There is scarcely anything which the understanding can know about God, but the will can love Him most deeply. Let a man imprison himself within himself, in the centre of his soul, where the image of God is, and there let him wait upon Him, as one listens to another speaking from some high tower, or as though he had Him within his heart, and as if in all creation there were nothing else save the soul and God. He should even forget himself and what he is doing, for, as one of the Fathers said, 'perfect prayer is that in which he who is praying is unaware that he is praying at all.'

And not only at the end of this exercise, but also at the middle, or in whatever part this spiritual slumber may overtake us when the understanding is, as it were, put to sleep by the will, we should make this pause and enjoy this benefit, and then, having tasted and digested this morsel, return to our labour. Just so the gardener, watering a patch of ground, turns off the hose when the ground is thoroughly watered, and allows the water to soak right into the earth and penetrate it. Then, when it has drained away and left the ground dry, he turns on the flow from the source again, so that it may receive more and more and be the better watered.

What the soul experiences at times like this, what light it rejoices in, what fullness and love and peace it receives, no words can express; for this is that peace that passes all understanding and all the happiness that this life can attain.

Some few there are so captivated by the love of God that hardly have they begun to think upon Him than immediately their inmost being melts at the thought of His sweet name. Such as these have as little need of reasonings or meditations to make them·love Him as has a mother or a bride to make her feast upon the thought of her son or her lover when people speak to her of him. And others, not only during the practice of prayer, but even apart from it, are so absorbed and immersed in God that they forget everything—even themselves—in Him. And if such absorption can often result from the frenzied dread of a lost soul, how much the more may it not be caused by the love of that infinite beauty, since grace is no less powerful than nature and guilt?

So, when the soul experiences this feeling, in whatever part of her prayer it may be, she should on no account set it aside, even though she should spend the whole time of the exercise in this way, and neither recite vocal prayers nor meditate as she had planned to do, unless such prayers were of obligation. For, as St. Augustine says, vocal prayer should be abandoned if at any time it were to impede devotion, and just so should meditation, if it were to impede contemplation.

Here, too, it is to be carefully noted that, just as we may leave meditation for affection, and thus mount from the lower to the higher, so, on the other hand, it will be well at times for us to leave affection for meditation, should the affection be so vehement that there were risk of peril to the health if one were to persevere in it. This often happens to those who devote themselves to these exercises without heeding·this counsel, and pursue them indiscreetly, attracted by the force of Divine sweetness. In such a case as this (says a Doctor) a good remedy is to induce an affection of compassion, by meditating for a little upon the Passion of Christ, or upon the sins and miseries of the world, to ease and relieve the heart.

TREATISE OF PRAYER AND MEDITATION, Part I, Chapter XII.

JUAN DE ÁVILA
1500—1569
(See p. 19, above)

E D I T I O N S. Apart from a small selection from the *Spiritual Letters*, made by the Benedictines of Stanbrook (*Letters of Blessed John of Ávila.* London, 1904), none of the works have been translated into English since the seventeenth century. Several editions of the complete works (e.g. *Obras*, ed. José Fernández Montaña, Madrid, 1901, 4 vols.), as well as of individual works, exist in Spanish.

S T U D I E S. N. González Ruiz: 'El Maestro Juan de Ávila y su Epistolario', in *Bulletin of Spanish Studies*, Liverpool, 1928, Vol. V, pp. 120-7, 154-8.

E. Allison Peers; 'Juan de Ávila,' in *Studies of the Spanish Mystics*, London, Vol. II, 1930, pp. 121-8, 419-21.

LETTER TO A RELIGIOUS, URGING HIM TO THE PERFECT LOVE OF GOD

Very Reverend Father: *Pax Christi*. Since it is not the pleasure of Our Lord Jesus Christ that I should be just now where I may enjoy the company of your Reverence and of your collegians as I should like, blessed be His Name. I bear it patiently, and I think this is no little penance for me, for it is a hard thing for a man to endure being separated from one he loves. And truly I have never so greatly desired the correction of your Reverence as I do now, for I think it would be of great service to Our Lord. But since all He does seems good to those that love Him, I will say a little in absence until God shall grant me your presence. I greatly desire, sir, that we should seek God, Who is our Good; and that not anyhow, but as one seeking a treasure which he desires, and for love of which he sells all he has, thinking himself rich in the possession of this

71

single thing in the place of many things which he had before.

O Lord God, in Whom our innermost heart may find rest! When shall we begin, I say not to love Thee, but even to wish that we may love Thee? When shall we have a desire for Thee that is worthy of Thee? When shall we be moved by truth rather than by vanity; by beauty rather than by ugliness; by quietness rather than by restlessness; by the Creator, so satisfying and all-sufficient, rather than by the creature that is poor and empty? And who, O Lord, shall open our eyes and make us realize that apart from Thee there is nothing that can satiate or abide? Who shall reveal to us something of Thyself, that we may be enamoured of Thee, and may run—nay, fly—so as to be for ever with Thee? Alas, that we are so far from God, and that it grieves us so little, scarcely causing us sorrow! Where are those sighs of deep affection which come from souls that have once tasted of God and then are withdrawn from Him a little? Where is that which David said in the hundred and thirty-first Psalm: Shall I give sleep to mine eyes, or slumber to my eyelids, until I find out a house for the Lord?

And we ourselves are this house, save when we lose ourselves in distractions among divers things: when we recollect ourselves in unity of desire and love, then do we find ourselves and are the creatures of God. I believe that the cause of our lukewarmness is, as one said, that he who has not tasted of God knows neither what it is to hunger, nor yet to be filled. And so we neither hunger for Him, nor do we find satisfaction in creatures, but are cold, indifferent, slothful and faint-hearted, without relish for the things of God and fit to be spewn forth by Him Who will have His servants, not lukewarm, but inflamed with the fire which He came to bring to the earth, and wills not but that it be kindled. And that it might be kindled He Himself was consumed by fire and burned upon the Cross, just as the red heifer was burned without the camp, that we ourselves might take that wood of the Cross, and kindle a fire with it and be warmed by it, thus returning some degree of love to Him Who has so greatly loved us, and considering how just a thing it is that we should be wounded by that sweet wound of love; since we see Him not only wounded by love, but killed by it.

It is right that we should be made captives by love for One Who for our sakes was delivered as a Captive into the hands of such cruel men. Let us enter the prison of our love for Him, since He entered the prison of His love for us, and for us became as a meek lamb before those who despitefully used Him. It was this bondage of love which made Him stay upon the Cross, for the ties and bonds of our love were far greater and stronger than the ropes and nails: these constrained His body, but love constrained His heart. Let our hearts, then, be bound with His love—the very bond of salvation—and let us desire no freedom which shall loose us from such bondage; for, as he that is not wounded by His love has no true health, so he that is not bound and in His prison has no true freedom.

So let us no longer resist Him; let us allow ourselves to be vanquished by His weapons—that is, His benefits—with which He would slay us that we may live with Him. He would fain burn us up, so that our old man, which is in the likeness of Adam, may be destroyed, and our new man, which is in the image of Christ, may be born through love. He would fain melt our hard hearts, so that, as on metal molten by heat is imprinted the image willed by the artificer, so we, softened by love which causes us to melt when we hear the Beloved's voice, may not resist Him, but be ready for Him to imprint upon us the image that He wills—that is, the image of Christ Himself, which is the image of love. For Christ is love itself and He commanded us to love one another, as He loved us. And St. Paul tells us that we should walk in love, even as Christ loved us and gave Himself for us, so that, if we love not, we are unlike Him, we have another countenance, we are not as He is, we are poor, naked, blind, deaf, dumb and

73

dead, for it is love alone that gives light to all things, and it is He Who has the spiritual care of our soul, which without Him is like a soulless body.

Let us love, then, reverend Father, and we shall live. Let us love, and we shall be like to God, and shall wound God, Who is wounded by love alone. Let us love, and God will be ours, since love alone possesses Him. Let us love and all things will be ours, for all will serve us, as it is written: All things work together for good to them that love God. If this love seems good to us, let us lay the axe of diligence to the root of our love of self and let us fell this enemy of ours to the ground.

SPIRITUAL LETTERS

ALONSO DE OROZCO

1500—1591

(See p. 20, above)

EDITIONS. None of Orozco's numerous works (*Obras*, Barcelona, 1882, 2 vols.) have been translated into English; seventeenth-century translations exist in French and Italian.

STUDIES. W. A. Jones: *Life of Blessed Alphonsus Orozco*, Philadelphia, 1895 (adapted from the biography of P. Tomás Cámara, Valladolid, 1882).

P. Ignacio Monasterio: In *Místicos agustinos españoles*, Madrid, 1929, Vol. I, pp. 142-66.

E. Allison Peers: 'Augustinian Mystics: Alonso de Orozco,' in *Studies of the Spanish Mystics*, London, Sheldon Press, Vol. II, 1930, pp. 191-218, 427-36.

OF THE LAST DEGREE OF CONTEMPLATION, WHICH CONSISTS IN THE CONTEMPLATION OF GOD IN HIMSELF

'This is the generation of them that seek the face of the God of Jacob.' These are they that ever seek the Lord and desire to see the face of Christ, the true Jacob. In this last degree, brother, our desire and intent attain their goal. For we must strive towards it, not merely that we may find our God in His image (which was the first degree), considering Him in ourselves; nor are we to follow in His footsteps, by contemplating Him in His creatures, which was the second degree. Still less have we to consider Him made man, and suffering for us upon the Cross, as in the third degree, but by a higher manner of contemplation we are to contemplate Him in His Essence and most perfect Being, without any kind of roundabout way.

Here the Eagle, as the prophet Ezekiel saw, must fly above itself. Two flights it must make: in the first it must fly higher than the man, the lion and the calf, which were three forms seen in company with the Eagle; the second is the flight of the soul above itself, casting aside all natural reason. By the form of the man which the prophet saw in that vision might be understood the first degree of contemplation, in which each may contemplate God in himself. By the form of the lion may be denoted the second degree, in which God is contemplated in His creatures. And by the similitude of the calf, which in the Law was a pure sacrifice, may be denoted the third degree, in which is contemplated God made man, and offering Himself on the Cross, a sacrifice for the sins of the world. By the eagle which flies higher we have now to understand this last degree of contemplation, in which are exercised those of whom the holy prophet David said that they seek not the Lord alone. This is contemplation according to the three degrees aforementioned; but they go farther, and, by a mighty effort, fix their eyes upon the sun, contemplating in that 'wheel' the wonderful perfection, and the Being, of their Creator, Who is called the Face of Jacob.

But I will warn thee, brother, that he who would see the face of that most powerful Wrestler, our boundless God, must first have wrestled with himself, and be a man perfect in the active life who has exercised himself for a while in these three aforementioned degrees of contemplation. For St. Gregory says: It is far better that he who feels himself unfit for contemplation should exercise himself humbly in the active life, for his whole life if need were, rather than presumptuously devote himself to contemplation, in which he may be led astray by some error, as his pride would merit. This is what our Redeemer said: 'If thy right eye offend thee, pluck it out, for it is better for thee to go to Heaven with one eye than to hell with both.' Far better will it be for thee to be saved in the active life (which is, as it were, the left eye) than to presume to follow the contemplative life feeling thyself unfitted for it, and thus losing the merit of the one life and also of the other.

MOUNT OF CONTEMPLATION, Chapter XII.

LUIS DE GRANADA
1504—1588
(See p. 18, above)

E D I T I O N S. Some twenty sixteenth- and seventeenth-century translations into English of works by Luis de Granada are extant, but there
is nothing modern. His complete works have been published in a
fourteen-volume critical edition in Spanish (*Obras*, ed. Fr. Justo Cuervo,
Madrid, 1906-8).

S T U D I E S. Azorín: Essays in *Los Dos Luises*, Madrid, 1921, and
De Granada a Castelar, Madrid, 1922.

P. Justo Cuervo: *Biografía de Fray Luis de Granada*. Madrid, 1895.

E. Allison Peers: 'Luis de Granada,' in *Studies of the Spanish
Mystics*, London, Sheldon Press, Vol. I, 1927, pp. 31-76, 422-30.

P. Maximino Llaneza has published a *Bibliografía del V.P.M. Fray
Luis de Granada* (Salamanca, 1926-8, 4 vols.).

A PRAYER FOR UNION WITH GOD
IN LOVE

Who, then, Lord, is all my happiness, and my final goal,
but Thyself? Thou, Lord, art the term of my journeyings,
the port of my sailings, the end of all my desires. How,
then, shall I not love Thee with this love? Fire and air
break through the mountains and make the earth tremble
when they are beneath it and are rising to their native place.
How, then, shall I not break through all the creatures, and
cleave a path through steel and through fire, until I reach
Thee, Who art the place of my rest? A vessel will go only
into the receptacle for which it was made. Then, since my
soul is a receptacle which Thou didst create for Thyself,
how can it be content with aught but Thee? Remember,
then, my God, that, as I am for Thee, so also art Thou
for me. Flee not, then, from me, Lord, that I may be able
to attain to Thee. Very slowly do I journey; oft do I halt
on the way and turn backward. Weary not, Lord, of waiting for one who follows Thee not with equal step.

Oh, my God and my salvation, why do I so often halt?
Why do I not run with supreme swiftness to my Supreme
Good, in whom all good things are contained? What can
man desire that is not better found in this ocean of goodness than in the muddy little pools of creatures? Men love
riches, love honours, long life, tranquillity, wisdom, virtue,
joys and such-like things, and with so great a love do they
love them that many a time for their sakes they are ruined.
O foolish and base lovers, that love the shadow and despise
the substance, that go to fish in dirty pools and forget the
sea! If each of these things deserves to be loved for itself,
how much more should He be loved Who is of greater
worth than all of them together? If the father of the prophet
Samuel could say with truth to his wife, who was weeping
because she had no sons, that he alone was worth more
to her than ten sons, with how much more truth, O Lord,
wilt Thou say to the soul of the righteous man that Thou
art worth more to him than all the creatures? For what
rest, what riches, what joys can be found in the creatures
that are not infinitely more abundant in the Creator? The
joys of the world are carnal, vile, deceptive, brief and
transitory. They are won with labour, held with anxiety
and lost with grief. They endure but a little, yet do great
harm. They inflate the soul and feed it not, deceive it and
sustain it not; and therefore they make it not happier but
more wretched, thirstier, farther from God and from itself,
and in condition more like to the beasts. Therefore said
St. Augustine: Miserable is the soul round whose affections
are entwined things below, for when they are taken from
him he is torn to pieces. And then he comes to realize his
misery through experience of the harm which these affections make him suffer—though he was miserable, too,
before he suffered it. But Thyself, O Lord, none can lose,
save he who leaves Thee of his own free will. He that
loves Thee enters into the joy of his Lord, and he will have
naught to fear, but will rather be at peace in Him Who is
peace eternal. . . .

May I love Thee, then, O Lord, with the straitest and most

fervent love. May I stretch out mine arms—that is, all my affections and desires, to embrace Thee, sweetest Spouse of my soul, from Whom I hope for all good. The ivy clings so closely to its tree that the whole of it seems to be throwing out arms wherewith to grasp the tree more closely, for by means of this support it mounts on high and attains what to it is perfection. And to what other tree must I cling than to Thyself, that I may grow and attain what I lack? This plant clinging to the trees grows not more, nor throws more widely its lovely branches than the soul grows in virtues and graces when it clings to Thee. Then why shall I not love Thee with all my soul, and strength, and powers? Help me, my God and my Saviour, and raise me on high in quest of Thyself, for the grievous weight of this mortal life drags me downward. Thou, Lord, Who didst mount the tree of the Cross to draw all things unto Thee; Thou Who with so vast a love didst unite two such different natures in one Person, to make Thyself one with us: do Thou be pleased to unite our hearts with Thyself by so strong a bond of love that they may at last become one with Thee, since Thou didst unite Thyself with us that we might be united with Thyself.

CONSIDERATIONS OF THE DIVINE PERFECTIONS, Part V, Chapter I.

ST. TERESA OF JESUS
1515—1582
(See pp. 21-3, above)

E D I T I O N S. The *Complete Works of St. Teresa of Jesus* (excluding
the *Letters*) have been translated in three volumes (London, Sheed and
Ward, 1946) and the *Letters* in two volumes (London, Burns Oates,
1951). The text used is that of P. Silverio de Santa Teresa's nine-volume
edition (Burgos, 1915-24). Of individual works there are earlier translations, published by Thomas Baker, by J. Dalton (1851 ff.), David
Lewis (1870 ff.), and the Benedictines of Stanbrook (1906 ff.).

S T U D I E S. Gabriela Cunninghame Graham's *Santa Teresa* (London,
Eveleigh Nash, 2nd ed., 1907) is still the fullest biography in English.
My *Mother of Carmel* (London, S.C.M. Press, 1945) is a briefer sketch,
as is the chapter (pp. 133-225: Bibliography, pp. 433-42) in *Studies of
the Spanish Mystics* (London, Sheldon Press, Vol. I, 1927). The early
Spanish biographies of Ribera (1590) and Yepes (1615) are still valuable.
A more modern Life is Mir's (*Santa Teresa de Jesús*, Madrid, 1912,
2 vols.). For her sources, see G. Etchegoyen's *L'Amour divin*
(Bordeaux, 1923); on her style, R. Hoornaert's *Sainte Térèse écrivain*
(Paris, 1922); English trans.: *St. Teresa in her writings* (London, Sheed
and Ward, 1931).

THE SIMILITUDE OF THE
WATERED GARDEN

The beginner must think of himself as of one setting out
to make a garden, in soil most unfruitful and full of weeds,
in which the Lord is to take His delight. His Majesty up-
roots the weeds and will set good plants in their place. Let
us suppose that this has already been done—that a soul
is determined to practise prayer and has already begun to
do so. With God's help, we have now to be good gardeners
and make these plants grow, and to water them carefully,
so that they may not die, but may produce flowers which
shall give out great fragrance and refresh this our Lord,
so that He may often come into the garden to take His
pleasure and have His delight among these virtues.

Let us now consider the way in which this garden can be watered, so that we may know what we shall have to do, how much labour it will cost us, if the gain will be greater than the labour, and for how long this labour must be borne. It seems to me that the garden can be watered in four ways: by taking the water from a well, which is hard work for us; or by a water-wheel and buckets, when the water is drawn by a windlass (I have sometimes drawn it in this way: it is not such a hard one as the other and gives more water); or by a stream or a brook, which waters the ground much better, for it saturates it more thoroughly and there is less need to water it often, so that the gardener's labour is much less; or by heavy rain, when the Lord waters it and it costs us no work at all, a way incomparably better than any of the others.

And now I come to my point, which is the application of these four methods of watering by which the garden is to be kept fertile and without which it will be ruined. In this way I think I can explain something about the four degrees of prayer to which the Lord, of His goodness, has occasionally brought my soul. May He also, in His goodness, grant me to speak in such a way as to be of some profit to one of those who commanded me to write this book, and whom in four months the Lord has brought to a point far higher than that which I have reached in seventeen years. He prepared himself better than I, and thus his garden, without labour on his part, is watered by all these four means, though he is still receiving the last watering only drop by drop; such progress is his garden making that soon, by the Lord's help, it will be submerged. I shall be glad for him to laugh at my explanation if he thinks it foolish.

Beginners in prayer, we may say, are those who draw the water from the well; this, as I have said, is very hard work, for it will fatigue them to keep their senses recollected, which is extremely difficult because they have been accustomed to a life of distraction. Beginners must accustom themselves to pay no heed to what they see or

hear, and they must practise this during hours of prayer;
they must go away by themselves and in their solitude think
over their past life—we must all do this, in fact, whether
we are at the beginning of the road or near its end. There
are differences, however, in the extent to which it must be
done, as I shall show later. At first it causes distress, for
beginners are not always sure that they have repented of
their sins (though clearly they have, since they have determined to serve God so faithfully). Then they have to endeavour to meditate upon the life of Christ, which fatigues
their minds. Thus far we can make progress by ourselves
—with the help of God, of course, for without that, as is
well known, we cannot think a single good thought.

That is what is meant by beginning to draw water from
the well—and God grant there may be water in it! But that,
at least, does not depend on us: our task is to draw it and
to do what we can to water the flowers. And God is so
good that when, for reasons known to His Majesty, perhaps
to our great advantage, He is pleased that the well should
be dry, we, like good gardeners, do all that in us lies, and
He keeps the flowers alive without water and makes the
virtues grow. By water here I mean tears—or at least, if
there are no tears, tenderness and an interior feeling of
devotion.

What, then, will a person do here who finds that for many
days he experiences nothing but aridity, dislike and dis-
taste, and has so little desire to go and draw water that he
would give it up entirely did he not remember that he is
pleasing and serving the Lord of the garden; if he were not
anxious that all his service should not be lost, to say nothing
of the gain which he hopes for from the hard work of continually lowering the bucket into the well and then drawing
it up without water? It will often happen that, even for that
purpose, he is unable to lift his arms—unable, that is, to
think a single good thought, for working with the understanding is of course the same as drawing water from the
well.

What, then, as I say, will the gardener do here? He will

rejoice and take new heart and consider it the greatest of favours to work in the garden of so great an Emperor; and as he knows that he is pleasing Him by doing so (and his purpose must be to please, not himself, but Him), let him render Him great praise for having placed such confidence in him, because He sees that, without receiving any recompense, he is taking such great care of that which He had entrusted to him; let him help Him to bear the Cross and remember how He lived with it all His life long; let him not wish to have his kingdom on earth or ever cease from prayer; and so let him resolve, even if this aridity should persist his whole life long, not to let Christ fall with His Cross.

LIFE, Chapter XI.

THE SIMILITUDE OF THE SILKWORM

You will have heard of the wonderful way in which silk is made—a way which no one could invent but God—and how it comes from a seed which looks like tiny peppercorns (I have never seen this, but only heard of it, so if it is incorrect in any way the fault is not mine). When the warm weather comes, and the mulberry trees begin to put on leaf, this seed shows signs of life; until it has this sustenance, on which it feeds, it is as dead. The silkworms feed on the mulberry leaves until they are full-grown, when people put down twigs upon which, with their tiny mouths, they start spinning silk, and make themselves very tight little cocoons, in which they bury themselves. And then the worm, which was large and ugly, comes out of the cocoon a beautiful white butterfly.

Now, if no one had ever.seen this, and we were only told about it as if it belonged to the past, who would believe it? And what arguments could we find to support the belief that a thing as devoid of reason as a worm or a bee could

83

be diligent enough to work so industriously for our profit, and that in such an enterprise the poor little worm would lose its life? This alone, sisters, even if I tell you no more, is sufficient for a brief meditation, for it will enable you to reflect upon the wonders and the wisdom of our God. What, then, would it be if we knew the properties of everything? It will be a great help to us if we occupy ourselves in thinking of these wonderful things and rejoice in being the brides of so wise and powerful a King.

But to return to what I was saying. The silkworm is like the soul which takes life when, through the heat of the Holy Spirit, it begins to utilize the general help which God gives us all, and to employ the remedies He left in His Church—such as the frequent use of confession, the reading of good books and the hearing of sermons, which are the remedies for a soul dead in negligences and sins and plunged into temptations. The soul begins to live and nourishes itself on this food, and on good meditations, until it is fully grown—and that is what concerns me now: the rest is of little importance.

When it is fully grown, then, as I said first of all, it starts to spin its silk and to build the house in which it is to die. This house may be understood here to mean Christ. I think I read or heard somewhere that our life is hid in Christ, or in God (for that is the same thing), or that our life is Christ. (Whether this be so or not is little to my purpose.)

Here, then, daughters, you see what we can do, with God's favour. May His Majesty Himself be our Mansion, as He is in this Prayer of Union which we ourselves spin. When I say He will be our Mansion, and we can construct it for ourselves and hide ourselves in it, I seem to be suggesting that we can subtract from God, or add to Him. But do not imagine we do that. We can neither subtract from God nor add to Him, but we can subtract from, and add to, ourselves, just as these little silkworms do! And, before we have finished doing all that we can in that respect, God will take this tiny achievement of ours, which is nothing at all, unite it with His greatness and give it such

84

worth that its reward will be the Lord Himself. And as it is He Whom it has cost the most, so His Majesty will unite our small trials with the great trials which He suffered, and make both of them into one.

To work, then, my daughters! Let us hasten to perform this task and spin this cocoon. Let us renounce our self-love and self-will, and our attachment to earthly things. Let us practise penance, prayer, mortification, obedience, and all the other good works that you know of. Let us do what we have been taught; and we have been instructed about what our duty is. Let the silkworm die—let it die, as in fact it does when it has completed the work which it was created to do. Then we shall see God and shall be as completely hidden in His greatness as that little worm is in its cocoon. Note that, when I speak of seeing God, I am referring to the way in which, as I have said, He allows Himself to be apprehended in this kind of union.

And now let us see what becomes of this silkworm, for all that I have been saying about it is leading up to this. When it is in this state of prayer, and quite dead to the world, it comes out a little white butterfly. Oh, the greatness of God! To think that a soul should come out like this after being hidden in the greatness of God, and closely united with Him, for so short a time—never, I think, for as long as half an hour! I tell you truly, the very soul does not know itself. For think how different an ugly worm is from a white butterfly; it is just like that here. The soul cannot imagine how it can have merited such a blessing— whence such a blessing can have come to it, I mean, for it knows quite well it has not merited it at all. It finds itself so anxious to praise the Lord that it would gladly be consumed and die a thousand deaths for His sake. Then it finds itself longing to suffer great trials and unable to do otherwise. It has the most fervent desires for penance, for solitude, and for everybody to know God. And therefore, when it sees God being offended, it becomes greatly distressed. In the following Mansion we shall treat of these things further and in detail, for, although the experiences of this

Mansion and of the next are almost identical, their effects become much more potent; for, as I have said, if after God comes to a soul here on earth it strives to progress still more, it will experience great things.

So you should see the restlessness of this little butterfly —though it has never been quieter or more at rest in its life! Here is something to praise God for—namely, that it knows not where to settle and make its abode. By comparison with the abode it has had, everything it sees on earth leaves it dissatisfied, especially as again and again God has given it this wine which almost every time has brought it some new blessing. It sets no store by the things it did when it was a worm—that is, by its gradual weaving of the cocoon. It has wings now: how could it be content to crawl slowly along when it can fly? All that it can do for God seems slight to it by comparison with its desires. It even attaches little importance to what the Saints endured, knowing by experience how the Lord helps and transforms a soul, so that it seems no longer to be itself, or even like what it was. For the weakness which it used to think it had and which made penance hard for it is now turned into strength. It is no longer bound by ties of relationship, friendship, or property. Previously all its acts of will and resolutions and desires were powerless to loosen these and seemed only to bind them the more firmly; now it is grieved at having even to fulfil its obligations in these respects lest these should cause it to sin against God. Everything wearies it, because it has tried in vain to find true rest in the creatures.

INTERIOR CASTLE, Fifth Mansions, Chapter II.

THE SEVENTH MANSIONS

When His Majesty is pleased to grant the soul the favour of this Divine Marriage, He first brings it out into His own Mansion. And it is His will that it should not be as at other times when He has plunged it into these raptures, at which times I certainly think He unites it with Himself, as He also does in the Prayer of Union, which has been described above, although the soul does not think itself to be called to enter into its centre, as it is in this Mansion, but is affected only in its higher part. This matters little: in one way or another the Lord unites it with Himself, but He does this by making it blind and dumb, like St. Paul at his conversion, and by thus preventing it from having any sense of how or in what way that favour which it is enjoying comes; for the great joy of which the soul is then conscious is the realization of its nearness to God. But when He unites it with Himself it understands nothing: the faculties are all lost.

But here it is different. Our good God now desires to remove the scales from the eyes of the soul, so that it may see and understand something of the favour which He is granting it, although He does this in a strange way. It is brought into this Mansion by means of an intellectual vision and by a particular kind of representation of the truth by which the Most Holy Trinity reveals Itself to it, in all three Persons. First of all, the spirit becomes enkindled, and is illumined, as it were, by a cloud of the greatest brightness. It sees these three Persons, individually, and yet, by a wonderful kind of knowledge which is granted to it, realizes that all these three Persons are one Substance, and one Power, and one Knowledge, and one God alone; so what we hold by faith the soul may be said here to grasp by sight, although it is not seen by the eyes of the body or of the soul, for it is no imaginary vision. Here all three Persons communicate Themselves to the soul and speak to the soul and explain to it those words which the Gospel attributes to the Lord—that He and the Father and the Holy Spirit will come and dwell with the soul that loves Him and keeps His commandments.

Oh, God help me! What a different thing it is to hear and believe these words and to realize in this way how true they are! Every day this soul grows more amazed, for she feels that they have never left her, and perceives

87

clearly, in the way that has been described, that They are within her soul, deep down in her very inmost being. As she is not a learned person, she cannot explain how this is, but she feels within herself this Divine companionship.

You will think that, this being so, such a person will not remain her own mistress, but will be so completely absorbed that she will be unable to think of anything. On the contrary, as regards the service of God she is much more able to do so than before, and, when she has no other occupations, she still enjoys that happy companionship. Unless her soul fails God, I do not believe He will ever fail to give her a clear realization of His Presence. She is fully confident that God will not leave her, and that, since He has granted her that favour, He will not allow her to lose it. She may well think this, without ceasing to walk more cautiously than ever, so that she may not displease Him in anything.

The realization of this Presence is not always as complete—I mean as clear—as it is when it first comes, or on certain other occasions when God is pleased to grant the soul this consolation: were it so, the soul could not possibly think of anything else, or even live in the world. But, although she has not so clear a light, she is always aware that she has this companionship. We might liken her to a person who is in a very bright room with some other people, when suddenly the shutters are closed and everything becomes dark. The light by which they can be seen has been taken away, and, until it comes back, she will be unable to see them, yet she remains conscious that they are there. It may be asked if, when the light comes back and she looks for them again, she will be able to see them. To do so is not in her power; it depends on when it is Our Lord's will that the shutters of the understanding shall be opened. In never leaving the soul, and in willing that she shall be so clearly aware of this, He is showing her an exceeding great mercy.

It seems that the object of the Divine Majesty in granting the soul this wonderful companionship is to prepare her for more. For clearly it will be a great help to her in her progress toward perfection and in her losing the fear which she used sometimes to have of the other favours that He granted her, as has been said. The person referred to found herself better in every way; and, however much she was worried by trials and business matters, the essential part of her soul used never to move from the place where she dwelt. So in a sense she would feel that her soul was divided; and, when she was experiencing sore trials, soon after God had granted her this favour, she would complain of it, just as Martha complained of Mary, and sometimes she would say that her soul was always enjoying itself in that quiet, and leaving her with all her trials and occupations so that she could not bear it company.

This will seem nonsense to you, daughters, but it is what really happens. In reality, of course, the soul is undivided, and yet what I have said is not fancy, but a very usual thing. As I was saying, it is possible to observe things that take place interiorly, so that we realize that there is some kind of difference between soul and spirit, and a very clear one, although both are one. A very subtle division can be apprehended between them, which sometimes makes it seem that the operation of the one is as different from that of the other as are the respective joys which the Lord is pleased to give them. It seems to me, too, that the soul is a different thing from the faculties and that they are not one and the same. There are so many and such subtle things in the interior life that it would be an audacity in me to begin to describe them. But we shall see everything yonder if the Lord, of His mercy, grants us the favour of bringing us to that place where we can understand these secrets.

INTERIOR CASTLE, Seventh Mansions, Chapter I.

AN EXCLAMATION OF THE SOUL TO GOD

O life, life, how canst thou find sustenance when thou art

absent from thy Life? In such great loneliness, wherein dost thou occupy thyself? What dost thou do, since all thy deeds are imperfect and faulty? Wherein dost thou find comfort, O my soul, in this tempestuous sea? I grieve for myself, but still more do I grieve for the time when I lived without grief. O Lord, how sweet are Thy paths! And yet who will walk in them without fear? I am afraid to live without serving Thee, yet when I set out to serve Thee I find no way of doing so that satisfies me or can pay any part of what I owe. I feel that I would gladly spend myself wholly in Thy service, and yet, when I consider my wretchedness, I realize that I can do nothing good unless Thou give it me.

O my God and my Mercy! What shall I do, so as not to destroy the effect of the great things which Thou workest in me? Thy works are holy, just, of inestimable worth and of great wisdom: and Thou, Lord, art Wisdom itself. But if my mind busies itself with this, my will complains, for it would fain have nothing hinder it from loving Thee. And in themes of such surpassing greatness the mind cannot attain to a comprehension of the nature of its God; it desires to enjoy Him, yet knows not how, while it is confined within a prison as grievous as this of mortality. Everything hinders it, though at first it was aided by meditation on Thy greatness, wherein it can the better see the baseness of numberless deeds of its own.

For what reason have I said this, my God? To whom do I make my complaint? Who will hear me if not Thou, my Father and Creator? But what need have I to speak that Thou mayest understand my grief, since I see so clearly that Thou art within me? This is folly on my part. But ah, my God, how shall I be sure that I am not separated from Thee? O my life, that must be lived in such uncertainty about a thing so important! Who would desire thee, since the gain to be derived or hoped for from thee—namely, to please God in all things—is so unsure and so full of peril?

EXCLAMATIONS OF THE SOUL TO GOD, I.

DIEGO DE ESTELLA
1524—1578
(See p. 19, above).

(See p. 19, above).

EDITIONS. Translations of the *Devout Meditations* were twice published in the nineteenth century: *A Hundred Meditations on the love of God*, described as by the Jesuit Robert Southwell (London, 1873); and *Meditations on the Love of God*, trans. by H. W. Pereira (London, 1898).

STUDIES. E. Allison Peers: 'Franciscan Mysticism: Diego de Estella'. In *Studies of the Spanish Mystics*, London, Sheldon Press, Vol. II, 1930, pp. 219-49, 436-42.

In Spain, the first substantial work on Estella appeared for the fourth centenary of his birth, notably in *Archivo Ibero-Americano*, 1924, Año XI, pp. 1-278, 384-8, and in a volume by various authors, *Fray Diego de Estella y su cuarto centenario* (Estella, 1924).

HOW LOVE BEARS US TO GOD, AS TO OUR CENTRE

Very true is it, Lord, and very clearly proved by experience, that, as Thou art the Good of men, so by its nature the force of love inclines and bears man to Thee, as to its source and centre, though oftentimes he is borne against his nature towards other things contrarily to his true welfare and honour. For, as our nature ever leads us to one thing, so also does our whole will bear us to one thing, though through our power of free choice which we have it is capable of following many, and can turn, by its own power, in whatever direction it desires. For there is no constraint in the will as there is in nature—would that there were, my God, would that we were bound by constraint to Thee, so that even if we willed otherwise we could not help ourselves, and so might be united with Thee, even as, by Thy great mercy, we shall be united with Thee after this life!

91

Alas for the great miracle that I see among men—a disastrous miracle, sorely to be lamented. Wouldst thou not perchance think it a very great miracle if thou wert to see a huge cliff suspended in the air, or supported by a feather, or if a mighty river were rushing onward with great force and a scrap of paper were seen to be sufficient to impede it? Who could look upon such a thing without crossing himself for fear? Who would not be amazed and astonished? Then how can I be other than amazed at seeing men whom trivial things suffice to hinder, my Lord, from attaining to Thee? Strange is it indeed; my God, that a man in whose nature there is so great a force of gravity bearing him to Thee should be weighted down by such frivolities as those of earth!

We are pilgrims in this world, for so the Holy Scriptures call us, and we journey toward Thee, O Lord, as toward our own country, and to our souls' true native land, wherein, as the Apostle says, we live and move and have our being. And, whenever we sin, we are hindered and halt on the way; the great marvel, and the great wonder, is that such trivial things can hinder us. My love is the force that moves me. By love I am borne whithersoever I go. Wheresoever my love rests, thither goes my soul; and even as Thou, O Lord, hast given a stone such force that, as it falls, it will go toward its centre and natural place, even so hast Thou given the same force to our souls—namely, a desire for the highest Good, to the end that it may the more readily be drawn to Thee by this attraction. If this be so, then, O my good God, how can it be that every soul that Thou hast created doth not go toward Thee with great speed? And yet we see souls hanging and suspended from a breath of wind, bereft of all good thereby, yet laughing and content and at rest.

How is it possible that any creature capable of union with Thee should not go toward Thee with all its strength, O infinite Centre infinitely good, and hence of infinite attraction? What can detain a creature capable of reaching so great a Good? O great weight of sin which, laid upon the neck of mankind, weighs it down and causes it to sink to the ground, that it may not rise to its rightful sphere, for which it was created!

Of a truth, it is a greater miracle that souls should not mount up to their God by love, than that rocks should be raised up and suspended by a breath of wind that they may not fall to their Centre; or than that a mere slip of paper should impede the course of a rapid torrent rushing toward the sea. Who, indeed, could endure his life patiently if he knew clearly and distinctly of what great good he is being deprived and how much good he is losing? O most ungrateful veil of my flesh, of how much joy dost thou deprive me! Who can hinder me from tearing and rending thee with my own hands, so that I may go and behold my God, and enjoy Him, and find my rest in Him? Oh, of how many pleasures and of what great happiness am I bereft because of thee! And, what is worse, how do I suffer thee, how do I laugh and remain at ease, well knowing, and seeing, and perceiving all this, and do not rather weep and groan, for days and nights, as would be just, over this my exile and blindness and pitiable plight?

How can I practise so evil and ungrateful a form of patience but that the veil is set between me and God, and that a fleshly cloud obstructs the sun's brightness from shining in my soul? Remove this veil which hinders me, and thou shalt see with what force my soul will travel toward its centre. Consider the souls of the saints, that are already loosed from this veil and are free: with what swiftness and lightness do they journey toward their God! Who can hinder them? Who can keep them back? Who can exile them from their rightful place? For therein is full and perfect rest; therein is eternal satisfaction for all the soul's restless desires.

DEVOUT MEDITATIONS ON THE LOVE OF GOD, Chapter IX.

LUIS DE LEÓN
1528—1591

(See pp. 20-1, above)

E D I T I O N S. *Lyrics of Luis de León*, trans. Aubrey F. G. Bell (Spanish and English texts). London, Burns Oates, 1928. *The Names of Christ*. Selections only, trans. by a Benedictine of Stanbrook. London, Burns Oates, 1926. A convenient modern edition of the complete works, in Spanish (*Obras completas castellanas*), will be found in the Biblioteca de Autores Cristianos (Madrid, 1944).

S T U D I E S. Aubrey F. G. Bell: *Luis de León, a study of the Spanish Renaissance*. Oxford, Clarendon Press, 1925. (The most substantial study on Luis de León in any language).

Adolphe Coster: *Luis de León*, in *Revue Hispanique*, Paris, New York, 1921-2, Vols. LIII, LIV, pp. 1-346.

W. J. Entwistle: 'Fray Luis de León's life in his lyrics: a new interpretation'. In *Revue Hispanique*, 1927, Vol. LXXI, pp. 176-224.

James Fitzmaurice-Kelly: *Fray Luis de León*. Oxford University Press, 1921.

E. Allison Peers: 'Luis de León,' in *Studies of the Spanish Mystics*, London, Sheldon Press, Vol. I, 1927, pp. 289-344, 449-60.

THE HEAVENLY LIFE

Fair land of radiant light,
Fields of the blest, to winter's frost unknown
And the sun's scorching might;
Soil ever newly sown,
Bearing eternal joy unto its own:

See the Good Shepherd come!
Snow-white and purple blooms enwreathe His head,
As to their heavenly home,
To fields well-waterèd,
Staffless and slingless His lov'd flocks are led.

94

He leads His sheep on high
Till, glad at heart, their pasture-land they view,
Where roses cannot die
And flow'rs are fresh with dew,
For ever cropp'd and yet for ever new.

Within the mountain's fold,
Faithful, He bathes them in the torrent's flood,
Laves them in joy untold,
Gives them abundant food:
Shepherd and Pasture He, and all their Good.

And when at length the sun
Has reached the zenith of his mighty sphere,
The hour of rest begun,
He to His flock draws near,
And with sweet sound delights His sacred ear.

He strikes the sonorous lyre,
And lo! the soul thrills to its deathless strain!
Dissolving in its fire,
It counts pure gold but vain,
Plunging within it ever and again.

O sound! O voice divine!
Might some faint note of this descend to me,
Transport my will in Thine,
Unite it utterly
Until it blend, O heavenly Love, in Thee!

Dear Love, did I but know
The pasture where Thy noontide rest would be,
I'd break my toils below,
And never stray from Thee,
But with Thy flock remain, for ever free.

THE BIRTH OF CHRIST IN THE SOUL

The birth of the soul in Christ signifies properly that the stain of sin, which made the soul appear in the likeness of the devil, is taken away, and that we receive the grace and the righteousness which God implants in us and which is like an image of Christ, so that we appear in His likeness. But the birth of Christ in us is not only that the gift of grace comes to the soul, but that the very Spirit of Christ comes and is united with it—is diffused throughout it, indeed, as if He were soul of its soul. And thus, diffused and as it were absorbed by it, this Spirit takes possession of its faculties and powers, not fleetingly or in haste, nor merely for a short time as happens in the glories of contemplation and in the raptures of the spirit, but abidingly and with a settled peace, like that of the soul reposing in the body. Christ Himself speaks in this way of it: 'He that loveth Me shall be loved of My Father, and We will come unto him and make Our abode in him.'

So, then, we are born in Christ when we receive His grace and grow in its likeness; but Christ is born in us when He comes through His Spirit to dwell in our souls and bodies. When He comes to dwell, I mean, and not only to bring joys and favours. So, although Marcelo told us yesterday of how we are born in God, there remains room to-day to tell of the birth of Christ in us. . . . Let us first say in how different a manner He dwells in the soul when He reveals Himself in prayer; and afterwards we will tell how and when Christ begins to be born in us, and of the strength which this birth and life of His within us bring, and of the degrees and stages of its growth.

First of all, then, between that advent and union with ourselves of the Spirit of Christ which we call His birth and His appearances to the souls of the righteous and the proofs of His presence which He gives in prayer, the principal difference is this. In this that we call His birth, the Spirit of Christ is united with the essence of the soul

96

LUIS DE LEÓN

and begins to work His virtue upon it, embracing it closely
without its perception or knowledge. And then He rests,
hidden as it were in its centre, as Isaiah says: 'Sing and
rejoice, O daughter of Zion, for the Lord of Israel is within
thee.' And from within its depths, as He rests there, He
diffuses the rays of His virtue through it and moves it
secretly. And by this movement and the obedience of the
soul thus moved, it gradually becomes a more spacious
dwelling, a larger room and a room more fitly prepared.
 But in the enlightenment and the consolations which
come through prayer, all the business of Christ is with the
faculties of the soul—the understanding, the will and the
memory. Sometimes He passes farther, even to the bodily
senses, and communicates Himself to them in diverse and
wondrous ways, to the extent to which these feelings are
possible to the human body. So entirely is the soul overwhelmed with the abundance of sweetness that the over-
plus passes to its companion (the body). For this reason
these periods of enlightenment and consolation, or this joyful union of the soul with Christ in prayer, is of the nature
of a lightning flash: I mean, it shines out, and is quickly
gone. For our faculties and our feelings, while this mortal
life endures, are absolutely compelled to busy themselves
with other thoughts and cares, without which a man does
not live, nor can he nor should he live.

And together with this difference there is another. In the
union of the Spirit of Christ with our spirits, which we call
the birth of Christ, His Spirit is as a soul calling to our soul,
and does within it the work of a soul, moving it to act as
it ought in all that offers, inspiring it with the impulse to
be up and doing and so working in it and moving it that
by its aid the soul works together with it. But in the
presence of Christ which He reveals to the faithful in
prayer, when He gives them joy and enlightenment, the
greater part of the soul and its faculties are at rest, and
He alone produces secretly in them a repose and a well-
being which surpass all description. And thus the first is
a living union, while the second brings delight and favour;

the one is existence and life, the other that which makes life sweet; in the one, the soul is inhabited by God and becomes like to God, in the other it tastes something of His felicity. The first, then, is given abidingly and for ever, because if it fails there is no life at all, while the second is given briefly and fleetingly, being a thing more of favour than of need, and because this life is given us for work, but this delight, so long as it lasts, turns us away from work and in its stead gives fruition.

NAMES OF CHRIST. Book III: *Son of God.*

LOVE AND UNITY

For love, as you were saying just now, Juliano and Sabino, is unity, or its whole office is to bring about unity; and the greater and better the unity, the greater and more excellent the love; whence it follows, without the least doubt, that the more the special ways in which two persons are as one to each other, the more love for each other will they have.

Now if in us there be both flesh and spirit, and if in so many ways Christ unites His Spirit with ours, stamping it with His likeness, communicating to it His strength, and shedding abroad in it His own Spirit, does it not seem to you undeniable, Juliano, either that His love to us is lacking in something, or that His Body also is united with ours, in so far as it is possible for two bodies to be united? And who will dare to set bounds in this respect to His love, which in all other respects is so exceeding great toward us? Again, I ask: Is it possible for God to accomplish this union? Or, if it be accomplished, does it not proclaim and exalt His love? Or does not God prize such exaltation? Clearly it is possible; most evidently it adds something of perfection; while undeniable and clearest of all is the fact that God prizes perfection in all that He does.

If this, then, is certain, how can it be doubted that God does all that can be done, and all that needs to be done, for the end He has in view? Christ Himself, praying to the

Father, says: 'Lord, I will that I and Mine own may be
one, even as Thou and I are one.' The Father and the
Son are one, not only because They have love toward each
other, nor because They are one both in will and in judgment, but because They are of one and the same substance,
so that the Father lives in the Son, and the Son lives through
the Father, and the life and being of both is the same.
Then if the similitude is to be as perfect as may be, it is
without doubt needful that we, the faithful, both as among
ourselves, and as between ourselves and Christ, should not
only be knit together and made one by that love which the
Spirit sheds abroad in our hearts, but that in our very
being, in body as in spirit, we should all be one, in so far
as is feasible and possible. It is needful that, being many
persons, as in fact we are, nevertheless by reason of the
same Spirit which dwells in our hearts, and of that same
and only Food which sustains us, we should all be one in
the Divine Body and Spirit, and closely united with each
other in both body and spirit, treated and constituted alike,
and that with the treatment and constitution proper to the
Divine Body and Spirit; and this is the highest degree of
union which can be attained or conceived as between things
so unlike in themselves.

So, then, just as a cloud which is penetrated by the force
and brightness of the sun's rays, filled and (if the word be
allowable here) saturated with light, is itself like a sun,
however it be looked at; just so, when Christ unites, not
only His virtue and light, but His very Body and Spirit,
with the faithful and just, and in some sort mingles His
very Soul with their souls, and His Body with their bodies,
in the way I have described, Christ looks out from their
eyes, speaks from their tongues, works through their senses;
their faces, their countenances, their movements are Christ,
Who thus occupies them wholly. So intimately does He
take possession of them that, though His Nature in no way
destroys or mars their own, there will be nothing seen in
them at the Last Day, nor will any nature be found in
them other than His Nature. There will be that one Nature

99

in all, and both He and they will be one and the same in
Himself.

Strong, indeed, Sabino, is that tie, and so fast a bond of
union that in nothing which Nature has formed or art in-
vented are the divers parts knit together with so fine and
so invisible a bond as this. Indeed, it is like the union of
matrimony, but so much the stronger and more excellent
as it is the straiter and more pure. It is purer than betrothal
or marriage after the flesh; and even so, or more, does it
excel such marriage in the intimacy of its union. For whereas in the one there is defilement of the body, in the other
there is deification both of soul and of flesh. Here there
is mutual affection between the wills of two persons; there
all is one will and one desire. Here the body of the one is
master of the other; there, without destruction of her substance, Christ the Spouse transforms His Bride into His
own Body, in the manner aforesaid. Here, men often stray;
there, they walk ever securely. Here, we find continually
anxiety and care, sworn foes of concord and union; there,
that rest and security which helps and favours the state
of those at one. Here, the union of two is to bring into the
world a third; there, one union leads to another, one embrace to another, and its fruit is oneness for evermore.

Here, happiness is but weak, delight of base alloy and
brief duration; there, both are so great that they submerge
alike body and soul—so noble, that they are glory—so
pure, that sorrow neither precedes nor follows them, nor
is joined nor mingled with them.

NAMES OF CHRIST. Book II: *Bridegroom.*

CHRIST THE PRINCE OF PEACE

Even did reason not prove, and were there no other way
of knowing how desirable a thing is peace, this glorious
spectacle of the heavens unveiled before us now, and the
harmony of the wondrous lights which shine in them afford
us sufficient testimony. For what is that but peace, or at

the least a perfect image of the same, which we now see in the heavens and which gives so much delight to our eyes? If peace, as St. Augustine briefly and truly concludes, is a tranquil order, or calm and steadfastness in that which good order requires, it is that very thing which this image reveals to us now. For here the host of the stars, placed as it were in order and arrayed in ranks, gives forth its wondrous light; each member inviolably keeps its place; none usurps the room of its neighbour nor hinders it in its office, far less, forgetful of its own, breaks the sacred and eternal law which Providence has given it. Rather do all of them, united among themselves, and as it were considerate of each other, the greater sharing their lights with the less, show signs of love, and in a manner do reverence to each other. All of them at certain seasons moderate their light and power, which they reduce to one peaceful uniformity of power, composed of divers parts and aspects, universal and powerful beyond all measure.

If we may so express it, they are not only a bright and lovely example of peace, but also a proclamation, a hymn of praise sung by an exceeding great multitude of voices, declaring to us how excellent are those virtues which peace contains in itself and which it brings to all things. The which voice and proclamation makes itself heard without noise of words in our souls, and its efficacy and persuasiveness are clearly manifest from the effect which there it makes. For our souls, perceiving how lovely and precious a thing is peace, begin to seek peace in themselves, and to set themselves throughly in order.

For, if we consider the secret things that pass within ourselves, we shall find that this order and harmony among the stars, as we contemplate it, brings rest to our souls; that, as our eyes are fixed intently upon the heavens, our desires and troubled affections, which surged tumultuously in our breasts by day, are gradually lulled to rest, we know not how; and that, sinking, as it were, to sleep, these desires are calmed, restored to their rightful place, and brought imperceptibly into subjection and harmony. We shall find,

101

too, that, as they are humbled and stilled, reason, which is chief and lord of the soul, rises above the rest, recovers its right and its strength, and, as if inspired by this glorious heavenly vision, conceives high thoughts, worthy of itself, and, in some sort mindful of its first beginning, sets all that is mean and vile in its proper place, and tramples it underfoot. Thus, with reason enthroned once more as empress of the soul, and its other parts reduced to their fitting place, the whole man is in an ordered and peaceful state.

But what of ourselves, who are reasonable beings? The rude and insensible works of creation, the elements, the earth, the air and the animals, order themselves and go to rest, when the sun sets and the resplendent host appears. See you not how silence is now over all things, as though they gazed in this most beauteous mirror, and forthwith were composed and at peace, returning to their places and offices, and contented with them?

Without any doubt peace is that good part which is in all things everywhere: wherever men see it they love it. And not peace alone, but the sight of its very image arouses our love, and makes us burn with longing to approach it, for we incline easily and without effort to our greatest good. And, indeed, if we confess the truth, as confess it we needs must, not only is peace sought generally by all, but it alone and naught else is so sought and desired and pursued. For all our work, so long as we live this life, and all our desire and labour, is directed towards the attainment of this blessing, peace. It is the goal to which all direct their thoughts, the blessing to which all aspire. For if the merchant takes a ship and ploughs the seas, it is to be at peace with his ambition, which ever importunes and assails him. And the labourer tilling the soil in the sweat of his brow seeks peace by driving away penury, so far as he may. So also he who follows pleasure, covets honour or cries out for revenge: all these, in their several aims, seek peace. For they pursue some good thing which they lack, or flee from some evil which molests them.

And because both that good thing which the desire pur-

102

sues, and the evil which is borne in fear and sorrow, disturb the repose of the soul, and are as enemies making war upon it, it is clear that all man's deeds are naught but efforts to flee from war and to pursue peace. And if this peace is our great and only good, who can be its Prince—that is, its chief fountain-head and source—save Him who is the author and the beginning of all that is good, Jesus Christ, our Lord and God? For if to possess peace is to be free from the evil which afflicts us and the desire which torments, and to enjoy quietness and rest, it is He alone Who can free our souls from fear, and enrich them in such a manner that there remains no more which they can desire.

NAMES OF CHRIST. Book II: *Prince of peace.*

PEDRO MALÓN DE CHAIDE
c. 1530—1589
(See p. 20, above)

EDITIONS. There are several Spanish editions of the *Conversión de la Magdalena* (e.g. Biblioteca de Autores Españoles, Vol. XXVII, Madrid, 1853, pp. 274-417; Barcelona, 1881. 2 Vols; Madrid, 1930. 2 vols.).
STUDIES. P. Ignacio Monasterio: In *Místicos agustinos españoles*, Madrid, 1929, Vol. I, pp. 230-48.

E. Allison Peers: In *Studies of the Spanish Mystics*, London, Sheldon Press, Vol. II, 1930, pp. 266-78, 446-7.

P. J. Pidal: In *Estudios literarios*, Madrid, 1890, Vol. II, pp. 143-75.

'ONE THING IS NEEDFUL'

Then, after the ascension of the Lord into Heaven, Mary, although forgiven, determined to withdraw into a desert place, where she might be alone and enjoy the contemplation of her Beloved. Ah, what sweet moments she would spend in that rugged land, among those crags! Carried away in spirit, as though she were already a citizen of Heaven and had thrown off that mortal vesture in which she was clothed, she quitted the earth, and soared in perfect freedom to the abode of her Beloved.

There she gazed upon those celestial mansions of the royal city of Jerusalem—a city filled with infinite light, its streets and squares thronged with the blessed who are citizens of that place. Through its gorgeous palaces thrilled music of ravishing sweetness, born of soft angelic voices which praise the great Prince of the World, without for a moment ceasing. When she considered the buildings erected by no human hand, but only by the will of that most beauteous God, she had no eyes for such great loveliness. She beheld the city, which was four square and of great immensity. Its foundations, as St. John tells in the Apocalypse, were of all the precious stones known to us here below, for they were of jasper and sapphire, chalcedony and emerald, jacinth and topaz, and of many other stones which are named in that book. The walls shone like the sun, so that no human eyes could look upon them. On each of the four sides were three gates, so that these were twelve in all, each of them a precious stone. The towers and battlements were crowned with crystal, and, as for the emeralds and rubies set in purest gold and illumined by the light and splendour of the true Sun which shines there, no human thought can reveal their unspeakable beauty. The ground, the streets and the squares of this blessed city are of the purest gold.

Herein dwells for ever springtime most fair, for bleak winter has been driven away. The fury of the winds cannot assail the lofty trees, nor the snow break down the tender branches with its weight. No sickly autumn strips the verdant groves of their leaves, for that word of David is fulfilled in them: 'Their leaf shall not wither.' For ever there dwells a mildness and a calm which preserves in the state of perfection all the freshness that Heaven holds. The flowers in the celestial meadows—white and blue and golden and of manifold and varied colours—surpass in their splendour the emeralds, rubies, bright pearls and Eastern stones. Here the rose is lovelier and more fragrant than in the gardens of Jericho, the springs are fairer than liquid crystal, the water is sweeter, the fruit more mellow to the taste.

O life that art life indeed! O glory that art glory alone! O royal city, whose citizens have great delight! None know the meaning of pain or sickness. Death comes not to thee, for all is life. There is no pain, for all is delight; no sickness, for God is true health. Blessed city, whose laws are of love, whose citizens are wholly possessed by love! In thee all love, their office is love, they know only how to love! One wish have they, one desire, one counsel. One thing they love, one they desire, one they contemplate, with one they are united. *Unum est necessarium.* One thing is needful.

CONVERSION OF THE MAGDALEN, § lxii.

JUAN DE LOS ÁNGELES
1536—1609
(See pp. 19-20, above)

E D I T I O N S. The standard edition of his works (*Obras místicas*, ed. P. Jaime Sala) was published (Madrid, 1912) as Vols. XX, XXIV, of the Nueva Biblioteca de Autores Españoles. None of these works has ever been translated into English.

S T U D I E S. J. Domínguez Berrueta: *Fray Juan de los Ángeles*, Madrid, 1927.

E. Allison Peers: In *Studies of the Spanish Mystics*, London, Sheldon Press, Vol. I, 1927, pp. 345-405, 460-2.

P. Antonio Torró: *Fray Juan de los Ángeles, místico-psicólogo*. Barcelona, 1924, 2 vols.

EJACULATORY PRAYER

PUPIL. A great thing must freedom of spirit be for this kind of prayer.

MASTER. I can most truly assure thee that without it neither the Kingdom of God, nor God Himself, can be within us. He who loses this freedom loses more than the value of earth and heaven, or of any other creature, or of all created things. For what do they all profit me, if my heart is bound to them, or to the very least of them, so that I cannot turn and raise it freely to the Creator?

PUPIL. What, then, are the conditions necessary to this prayer?

MASTER. The first and most important is purity of heart, without which we are neither fit nor disposed to receive the inflowing of Divine grace, through which our heart is established in God, and there is worked in us perfect abnegation and mortification of the passions and affections of humanity. And here I will add that the secret of the highest perfection, of grace and of glory, is perfect

106

abnegation and total resignation of ourselves in God, by which means we rise above ourselves, and are stripped of all attachment and in every way are brought into conformity with the will of God. Oh, love of self, how much harm dost thou cause to souls! So long as this love dwells in us it is for ever causing vice to spring up, and bringing forth evil thoughts, and exciting wrong inclinations and vain desires; which things separate us from God, stain our souls and disturb our inward peace, so that love of self is the greatest impediment to spiritual progress that can be found. But about this a great deal is said in the third dialogue, so no more will be set down here concerning either self-love or self-will.

Two or three counsels I will give thee as to freedom of aspiration. The first is that thou labour as much as thou canst to have thy heart free from conceits or images of creatures, representations and forms, and, most chiefly, from all inordinate affections. It is a great help toward this to flee from gossip and buffoonery, and from all occasions of curiosity and idleness, fair shows and vanities, and useless business and occupations, and from all that which the heart is fain to go after and cleave unto. Cut down all superfluity in eating and drinking, in dress and outward show, and thus thou wilt immediately and often and continually awaken the strength of desire in thy heart, multiplying thy desires of most pure and fervent love to the Lord.

But take note that herein there may be spiritual gluttony, and that marked injury may be done to the intellect if these prayers be made too impetuously and without moderation; in which respect many have corrupted themselves, taking more delight in these gifts of God than in God Himself. For which cause have thou ever care that thy intention be chaste, pure and god-like—that is, in conformity with the good pleasure and will of God, Whose glory only and alone is ever to be sought without respect to our own, as well in prosperity as in adversity.

107

Note, in the third place, the capacity and nobility of our soul, which, though it cannot operate with infinite power, since its virtue is finite, can at least reach out to infinity with its desire. God will not demand of thee that thou love Him with an infinite love, for this thou canst not; yet, since thy desire may stretch forth to things unattainable, God will have it stretch forth to the infinite—that is, to know no limit in its honour, love and desire of Him. So, then, in affective prayers thou hast not to consider the unattainableness of that which thou desirest, nor how infinitely it exceeds the virtue of thy soul and its powers of operation, but only whether that which thou desirest be lawful, and conducive to God's honour and glory.

And, when only impotence on our part impedes the realization of our desires, the desire will be crowned by God just as the operation would be crowned if we were able to perform it, and this belongs to one of the degrees of 'violent love' which Richard (of St. Victor) called insatiable, and which led St. Augustine to say that, if he were God, as the true God is, he would cease from being so that He might so become: this was desire for a thing unattainable, yet it was of great merit before God. This is that excess of love of the Bride, who says (Cant. i) that her virgins love the Beloved exceedingly. And of the man that feareth the Lord the Prophet said (Psal. iii) that he delighteth exceedingly in His commandments.

MANUAL OF PERFECT LIFE: Dialogue VI.

PREFACE TO THE 'CONSIDERATIONS ON THE SONG OF SONGS'

If any book needed the spirit of prophecy it would be this one; and not that alone, but also a knowledge of an infinitude of natural things and their properties, because

at every step these are introduced as the symbols of
things spiritual. In the first chapter alone, which has
occupied me for more than two years, I have met so many
difficulties that often I have wished to turn back from
the task, and much weariness and discouragement has
assailed me because I have become entangled in so vast
a maze. When I began to think of God as having a mouth,
and breasts, like those of women; a name, like oil poured
forth; robes more fragrant than precious ointments; a bed
that is green; houses of cedar-wood and cypress; cells and
retreats; the kiss of a bride; blackness and comeliness;
tents and shepherds; kids and sheep, and the like: then
I was quite beside myself, and lost all courage, and all
desire to write.

And the virtue of this is that in saying it I reprove myself, and compel myself to give a reason for my persistence
—nay, my daring—in endeavouring to undertake a task
so arduous and difficult, and so utterly beyond my powers.
I know that it suffices not to excuse me from blame if I
speak of my four-and-twenty years as a preacher, and my
constant exercise in the Scriptures; nor of the zeal for the
profit of souls which, through the mercy of God, I have
ever had; nor would it suffice me to be learned and versed
in many tongues, if such I were; nor to be as pious and
learned as St. Thomas, were I both. For that Saint feared
to essay this task—yea, even one so great as he—and all
the Saints feared it, though they were full of the knowledge of the Lord and of heavenly riches. Why, then, have
I committed myself to this task?

First, because of the entreaties of a friend, a weighty
man, and notable in learning, both human and divine.
Knowing my spirit, and how it is inclined to things of
affection and love, both from his reading of the *Triumphs*
and *Dialogues*, and from his acquaintance with me and
hearing of my sermons, he judged that great service would
be done to God, and no small benefit to the Christian
commonwealth, if I devoted myself to writing upon this
book, in which everything breathes forth and is fragrant

with love. For, as we said elsewhere, and as we shall in a more fitting place repeat, there is described here the chaste and pure love which is between Christ and the Church, or between Christ and the soul that has merited the name of Spouse and can say as in the opening verse: Let him kiss me with the kisses of his mouth.

The second consideration that urged me was an inclination and a love for this book, since the day that I was given licence to read in it by virtue of my office, a love so great that, even when I understood not what I read, I felt a particular delight and consolation of spirit as long as I was occupied in it. And this love grew with the years and was but strengthened by readings in the Saints who wrote of the book. . . .

It is a spiritual garden for the delight of Christian souls, who may gather the most fragrant posies of divers flowers for their consolation and pleasure. Here they will see what is meant by the love of God, its power and its obligations, the heights that it can reach, and the things from which it separates us. Here they will see the varying accidents of its nature, and the studies which it inspires—so different from those which in our days we see in persons called spiritual—and many will be disillusioned thereby and return to the truth.

I trust and am assured that I shall carry to an end this enterprise which for the glory of God and the edification of His Church I have begun; not that I am governed therein by my own meditations or my powers (for I am neither a prophet nor have in myself the grace of interpreting the Scriptures), but because of all that the Saints, and divers persons well approved, and men that are learned and versed in tongues have left in their writings. For, though I cannot have seen them all, I have seen the most part and the best, so that I write but little which is my own, and that little I write like a dwarf on the shoulders of a giant, upon which he is mounted, not by his own efforts, but because the giant has placed him there, serving him as a watchtower. Yea, I am indeed a dwarf and a pigmy in comparison with those who have preceded me in writing of this book, and, if I should discover and spy out more than they, it will be not because of my greater stature, but through the help of God and of themselves, who have given me light, and opened the way to everything.

My greatest care has been to seek after clearness, and to remove offences and occasions of stumbling from the simple, and thus it will be seen in the whole work that, besides being clear, the language is honest, chaste, sober, religious, giving occasion of evil to none. As touching the exposition of difficult passages, I give the opinions of all, when they are partially or wholly unlike, and choose that which I judge to be the best, which is ever that which touches the soul most nearly and ministers to good living. Especially as regards prayer and contemplation I extend myself most when occasion offers, for I desire that this book may come into the possession of spiritual persons whom I set often in right ways, and give admirable expositions to aid them in their desire, if such they have, to make progress in mystical theology and communion with their God, through the exercises of free, fruitive and seraphic love, which is the foundation of these Songs.

CONSIDERATIONS ON THE SONG OF SONGS. Preface.

ST. JOHN OF THE CROSS
1542—1591
(See pp. 23-4, above)

E D I T I O N S. The *Complete Works of St. John of the Cross* have been translated in three volumes (London, Burns Oates, 1934-5) from the text of P. Silverio de Santa Teresa's five-volume edition (Burgos, 1929-31). The earlier translations of David Lewis (1864 ff.) are admirably done, but from an inferior text. The poems are separately translated (Spanish and English text) as *The Poems of St. John of the Cross* (London, Burns Oates, 1947).

S T U D I E S. The literature is immense, and much has appeared since the publication of my bibliography in *Studies of the Spanish Mystics*, London, Sheldon Press, 1927-30, Vol. I, pp. 443-8, Vol. II, pp. 399-400. It includes three biographies:

P. Bruno: *St. John of the Cross*. London, Sheed and Ward, 1932.

P. Crisógono de Jesús Sacramentado: *Vida in Vida y Obras* (Biblioteca de Autores Cristianos), Madrid, 1946 (2nd ed., 1950).

E. Allison Peers: *Spirit of Flame*. London, S.C.M. Press, 1943.

Other outstanding works are:

Dámaso Alonso: *La Poesia de San Juan de la Cruz.* Madrid, 1942.

Jean Baruzi: *Saint Jean de la Croix et le problème de l'expérience mystique*. Paris, 1924.

Bede Frost: *St. John of the Cross*. London, Hodder & Stoughton, 1937.

R. Hoornaert: *L'Ame ardente de Saint Jean de la Croix*. Bruges, Desclée, 1928 (English trans. by Algar Thorold: *The Burning Soul of St. John of the Cross*, London, Burns Oates, 1931).

C. H.: *The Mystical Doctrine of* St. John of the Cross. London, Sheed and Ward, 1934.

E. Allison Peers: In *St. John of the Cross*, etc., London, Faber & Faber, 1946, pp. 11-53.

Robert Sencourt: *Carmelite and poet*. London, Hollis & Carter, 1944.

DARK NIGHT OF THE SOUL

Upon a darksome night,
Kindling with love in flame of yearning keen
—O moment of delight!—
I went, by all unseen,
New-hush'd to rest the house where I had been.

Safe sped I through that night,
By the secret stair, disguisèd and unseen
—O moment of delight!—
Wrapt in that night serene,
New-hush'd to rest the house where I had been.

O happy night and blest!
Secretly speeding, screen'd from mortal gaze,
Unseeing, on I prest,
Lit by no earthly rays,
Nay, only by heart's inmost fire ablaze.

'Twas that light guided me,
More surely than the noonday's brightest glare,
To the place where none would be
Save one that waited there—
Well knew I whom or ere I forth did fare.

O night that led'st me thus!
O night more winsome than the rising sun!
O night that madest us,
Lover and lov'd, as one,
Lover transform'd in lov'd, love's journey done!

Upon my flowering breast,
His only, as no man but he might prove,
There, slumbering, did he rest,
'Neath my caressing love,
Fann'd by the cedars swaying high above.

When from the turret's height,
Scattering his locks, the breezes play'd around,
With touch serene and light
He dealt me love's sweet wound,
And with the joyful pain thereof I swoon'd.

Forgetful, rapt, I lay,
My face reclining on my lov'd one fair.
All things for me that day
Ceas'd, as I slumber'd there,
Amid the lilies drowning all my care.

SPIRITUAL CANTICLE

Whither hast vanishèd,
Beloved, and hast left me full of woe,
And like the hart hast sped,
Wounding, ere thou didst go,
Thy love, who follow'd, crying, high and low?

Ye shepherds, soon to be
Among those sheepcotes on the hillside high,
If ye perchance should see
Him that I love pass by,
Say to him that I suffer, grieve and die.

I'll seek my love straightway
Over yon hills, down where yon streamlets flow.
To pluck no flowers I'll stay;
No fear of beasts I'll know;
Past mighty men, o'er frontier-grounds I'll go.

QUESTION TO THE CREATURES
You forest, thicket, dene,
Which my belovèd set in close array;
You meadow-land so green,
Spangled with blossoms gay,
Tell me, oh, tell me, has he pass'd your way?

ANSWER OF THE CREATURES
Rare gifts he scatterèd
As through these woods and groves he pass'd apace,
Turning, as on he sped,
And clothing every place
With loveliest reflection of his face.

BRIDE
O that my griefs would end!
Come, grant me thy fruition full and free!
And henceforth do thou send
No messenger to me,
For none but thou my comforter can be.

114

The creatures, all around,
Speak of thy graces as I pass them by.
Each deals a deeper wound
And something in their cry
Leaves me so raptur'd that I fain would die.

How do I still draw breath
Since 'tis no life at all, this life I know?
These arrow-wounds deal death
That do torment me so
And with fair thoughts of thee increase my woe.

Why piercedst thou this heart
And heal'dst it not upon the selfsame day?
Why usedst robbers' art
Yet leavest thus thy prey
And tak'st it not eternally away?

End thou my torments here,
Since none but thou can remedy my plight;
And to these eyes appear,
For thou art all their light
And save for thee I value not their sight.

Reveal thyself, I cry,
Yea, though the beauty of thy presence kill,
For sick with love am I,
And naught can cure my ill
Save only if of thee I have my fill.

O crystal spring so fair,
Might now within thy silvery depths appear,
E'en as I linger there,
Those features ever dear
Which on my soul I carry graven clear!

Withdraw thy gaze apart,
For, lo! I soar aloft.

ST. JOHN OF THE CROSS

SPOUSE

Return, my love!
See where the stricken hart
Looks from the hill above
What time he hears thy beating wings, my dove!

BRIDE

My love is as the hills,
The lonely valleys clad with forest-trees,
The rushing, sounding rills,
Strange isles in distant seas,
Lover-like whisperings, murmurs of the breeze.

My love is hush-of-night,
Is dawn's first breathings in the heav'n above,
Still music veil'd from sight,
Calm that can echoes move,
The feast that brings new strength—the feast of love.

Now blooms our nuptial bed,
Safe-hid from men by lions' fortress-lair,
With royal purple spread,
Builded all free from care,
Crown'd with a thousand golden scutcheons rare.

Youths that adore thy name
Follow thy footprints, for they sorely pine
To feel thy touch of flame,
To taste thy spicèd wine,
To be anointed with thy balm divine.

Within his secret store,
Of my belovèd drank I deep indeed.
Remembering then no more,
I roam'd this fertile mead,
My flock forgotten which I used to feed.

116

There gave he me his breast,
There taught me sweetest science of his own,
And I myself confest
His only, his alone,
Lavish'd my love upon him, keeping none.

My soul is well content
To serve her spouse with all her wealth and might.
Her days of toil full-spent,
Her flock now lost to sight,
— Love is her labour, love her sole delight.

So, should I ne'er again
Be seen or heard of on the common-ground,
Say that I roam'd in vain,
By bonds of true love bound,
— That I was lost, and that I now am found.

Of flowers and emeralds green,
Gather'd at coolest dawn on summer lea,
Garlands, my love, we'll glean
That joy to bloom for thee:
Bound with one golden hair of mine they'll be.

That golden hair one day
Thou saw'st as on my neck it lightly stray'd.
It bound thee then straightway;
A prisoner thou wert made
And wounded by my glance that on thee play'd.

When thou on me didst gaze
Thine eyes forthwith imprinted of their grace.
Then knew I love's amaze,
And, bolden'd in that place,
Straightway ador'd as I beheld thy face.

117

Ah, scorn me not, I pray,
For if, in truth, uncomely once was I,
Thy beauty came one day,
And cloth'd my misery:
Look then on me, thus shrouded, as I cry.

Drive us the foxes hence,
For, see! our vine has come at last to flower,
The while with roses dense
We twine our nuptial bower.
Let none disturb our groves at this glad hour.

Begone, chill northern blast!
Wind from the south, that wakenest love, be ours!
Breathe in us, winter past,
The fragrance of these bowers,
Where my belovèd pastures 'mid the flowers.

SPOUSE
Her entry she has made
Into the long'd-for garden, fair to sight.
Now rests she in its shade,
With fullness of delight,
Secure in the embrace of tranquil might.

Beneath the apple-flower
To plight my troth to thee, my love, I came.
My hand in that same hour
Pledg'd unto thee my name
In reparation of thy mother's shame.

Birds as ye take your wing,
Lion and hart and skipping fallow-deer,
River-bank, valley, spring,
Heats, breezes, mountains sheer,
Things that chase sleep and fill the nights with fear,

118

By siren's sweetest song
And pleasant lyre I conjure you to cease.
Let your tumultuous throng
No more assault our peace:
The Bride shall find in sleep secure release.

BRIDE

Daughters of Jewry, stay!
While choicest ambar-perfume doth invade
Rose-bowers and blossoms gay,
Rest in the outer glade
And come not to disturb our holy shade.

Hide thee, my lover dear,
And lift thine eyes until the hills they see.
Speak not, for none will hear;
Lo, where they company
With her that roams strange islands, far and free.

SPOUSE

See, where the milk-white dove
Bears to the ark the pledge of flood-freed ground,
And the comrade of her love
The turtle-dove has found
On verdant banks, with pastures all around.

So she who dwelt alone
In loneliness again has built her nest,
Guided alone by one,
Upon her lonely quest,
Who, lonely too, by love was sorely prest.

BRIDE

Belovèd, let us sing,
And in thy beauty see ourselves portray'd,
Where purest waters spring
Rippling o'er hill and glade;
Then enter farther in the forest's shade.

119

Mount we at last on high
Ev'n to the caverns of the rocky mine.
Enter we, thou and I,
Those secret haunts divine,
To drink of the pomegranate's ruddy wine.

There unto this thy dove
That which her soul has yearn'd for wilt thou show,
And there, dear life-of-love,
That blessing wilt bestow
Which once she has known and ever longs to know.

The gently moving air;
The sweetest song of Philomel the queen;
The forest wondrous fair
On a night of nights serene;
The flame consuming-fierce yet painless-keen.

None can behold us more
Nor e'en the Arch-Enemy can now appear.
For the long, long siege is o'er
And the horsemen, halting here,
Dismount and gaze upon the water clear.

NIGHT OF SENSE AND NIGHT OF SPIRIT

(i) NIGHT OF SENSE

This night, which, as we say, is contemplation, produces
two kinds of darkness or purgation in spiritual persons,
corresponding to the two parts of man—namely, sense
and spirit. And thus in the one night or purgation, which
is of sense, the soul will be purged and stripped according
to sense, by the subjection of sense to spirit; and in the
other night or purgation, which is of spirit, the soul will
be purged and stripped according to spirit, and subjected
and prepared for the union of love with God. The night

of sense is common and the lot of many; they are the beginners and of them we shall speak first. The night of the spirit is the portion of very few—namely, of those that are already practised and proficient: of them we shall treat later.

The first night or purgation is bitter and terrible to sense, as we shall now show. The second bears no comparison with it, for it is very awful to the spirit, as we shall show presently. Since the night of sense is first in order, and comes first, we shall begin by saying something about it, but briefly, since there is more written about it, as of a thing that is commoner; and we shall pass on to treat more fully of the spiritual night, since very little has been said of this, either in speech or in writing, and very little is known about it by experience.

As the manner in which these beginners in the way of God behave is ignoble, and is considerably affected by their love of self and their own inclinations, as has been explained above, God desires to lead them farther. He seeks to bring them out of that ignoble manner of love to a higher degree of love for Him, to free them from the ignoble exercises of sense and reasoning (by means of which, as we have said, they go in search of God so unworthily and in so many ways that are unbefitting) and to lead them to a kind of spiritual exercise in which they can commune with Him more abundantly and are more completely freed from imperfections. For they have for some time now been treading the path of virtue and been persevering in meditation and prayer, whereby, through the sweetness and pleasure that they have found therein, they have lost their love for things of the world and gained some measure of spiritual strength in God; this has enabled them to a certain extent to refrain from creature desires, so that for God's sake they are now able to suffer a light burden and a little aridity without regretting the better days when they found things more pleasant. When they are going about these spiritual exercises with increasing delight and pleasure, and when they think the

121

sun of Divine favour is shining on them more brightly, God turns all this light they are enjoying into darkness, and shuts against them the door and the source of the fresh spiritual water which they were tasting in God whensoever and for as long as they desired. (For, as they were weak and tender, no door was closed to them, as St. John says in the Apocalypse, iii, 8.)

He leaves them, then, completely in darkness, so much so that with their sensible imagination and meditation they know not where to betake themselves. For they can make no progress in meditation, as they were in the habit of doing before, their inward senses being overwhelmed by this night, and left in a state of such aridity that not only do they experience no pleasure and consolation in the spiritual things and good exercises in which they were accustomed to find their delight and pleasure, but, on the contrary, they find these things insipid and bitter. For, as I have said, God sees that they have grown a little, and are becoming strong enough to lay aside their swaddling clothes. So He takes them from His gentle breast, sets them down from His arms and teaches them to walk on their own feet. This makes them feel very strange, and they think everything is going wrong with them.

To recollected persons this generally happens at an earlier stage than it does to others, inasmuch as they are freer from occasions of backsliding, and their desires are quicker to turn from the things of the world, which is what is needful if they are to begin to enter this blessed night of sense. Not much time, as a rule, passes after they have taken their first steps before they begin to enter this night of sense; and the great majority of them do in fact enter it, for they will generally be seen to fall into these aridities.

DARK NIGHT OF THE SOUL. Book I, Chapter VIII.

(ii) NIGHT OF SPIRIT

This dark night is an inflowing of God into the soul,

122

which it purges of its ignorances and imperfections, habit-
ual, natural and spiritual; contemplatives call it infused
contemplation, or mystical theology. Here God teaches the
soul secretly and instructs it in perfection of love, without
its doing anything, or understanding the nature of this
infused contemplation. Inasmuch as it is God's loving
wisdom, it produces striking effects in the soul, which, by
purging and illumining it, He prepares for the union of
love with Him. So the same loving wisdom that purges the
blessed spirits and enlightens them is that which here
purges and illumines the soul.

But the question arises: Why is the Divine light (which,
as we say, illumines and purges the soul from its ignorances) here called by the soul a dark night? There are two
reasons, is the answer, why this Divine wisdom is not only
night and darkness to the soul, but also affliction and torment. The first is because the Divine Wisdom is so lofty
that it transcends the talent of the soul, and thus is darkness to it; the second is because of the soul's baseness and
impurity, which makes the Divine light painful and afflic-
tive to it, and also dark.

In order to prove the first point, we must assume a
certain philosophical doctrine, which says that, the clearer
and more manifest are Divine things in themselves, the
darker and more hidden are they to the soul naturally;
just as, the brighter is the light, the more it blinds and
darkens the pupil of the owl, and, the more directly we look
at the sun, the greater is the darkness which it causes in
our visual faculty, overcoming and overwhelming it through
its own weakness. In the same way, when this Divine light of
contemplation assails the soul which is not yet wholly enlightened, it produces spiritual darkness in it; for not only
does it overcome it, but likewise it overwhelms it and
darkens the act of its natural intelligence.

For this reason St. Dionysius and other mystical theo-
logians call this infused contemplation a ray of darkness—
that is to say, for the soul that is not enlightened and
purged—because the natural strength of the intellect is

123

conquered and overwhelmed by its great supernatural light.
This is why David said that near to God and round about
Him are darkness and cloud; not that this is really so,
but that it seems so to our weak understanding, which is
blinded and darkened by so dazzling a light, to which it
cannot attain. For this cause the same David explained
this, saying: 'Through the great splendour of His presence
passed clouds'—that is, between God and our understanding. And it is for this cause that, when God sends it out
from Himself to the soul that is not yet transformed, this
illumining ray of His secret wisdom causes thick darkness
in the understanding.

And it is clear that in these its beginnings this dark contemplation is also painful to the soul; for, as this infused
Divine contemplation has many excellences that are extremely good, and the soul that receives them, not being
purged, has many miseries that are likewise extremely bad,
it follows that, as two contraries cannot co-exist in one
subject, the soul must needs experience pain and suffering,
since it is the subject in which these two contraries war
against each other, working each against the other, by
reason of the purgation of the imperfections of the soul
which comes to pass through this contemplation. This we
shall prove inductively, as follows.

In the first place, because the light and wisdom of this
contemplation is most bright and pure, and the soul which
it assails is dark and impure, it follows that the soul suffers
great pain when it receives it in itself, just as, when the
eyes are dimmed by humours, and become impure and
weak, they suffer pain through the assault of the bright
light. And, when the soul is directly assailed by this Divine
light, its pain, which results from its impurity, is immense;
because, when this pure light assails the soul, in order to
drive out its impurity, the soul feels itself to be so impure
and miserable that it believes God to be against it, and
thinks that it has set itself up against God. . . .

The second way in which the soul suffers pain comes
from its weakness, natural, moral and spiritual, for, when

this Divine contemplation assails the soul with a certain force, in order to strengthen and subdue it, its weakness makes it suffer such pain that it nearly swoons away. This is especially so at certain times when it is assailed with somewhat greater force; for sense and spirit, as if beneath some immense and dark load, are in such great pain and agony that the soul would think it an advantage and a relief to die. . . .

A thing of great wonder and pity is it that the soul's weakness and impurity should now be so great that, though the hand of God is of itself so light and gentle, the soul should now feel it to be so heavy and so contrary, though it neither weighs it down nor rests upon it, but only touches it, and that mercifully, since He does this in order to grant the soul favours and not to chastise it.

DARK NIGHT OF THE SOUL, Book II, Chapter v.

'BREAK THE WEB OF THIS SWEET ENCOUNTER' [1]

For it is this web which hinders so important a business as this, since it is easy to reach God once the separating impediments and webs are taken away. These webs which must be broken if we are to possess God perfectly are reduced to three, namely: the temporal, which comprises every creature; the natural, which comprises the operations and inclinations that are purely natural; and the sensual, which comprises only union of the soul in the body, which is sensual and animal life, whereof St. Paul says: We know that if this our earthly house be dissolved we have a dwelling-house of God in the heavens. The first two webs must of necessity be broken in order that we may

---

-[1] The passage is a commentary on these words, which are a literal translation of the Spanish line, 'Living flame of love,' St. I, translated in verse, on p. 24, above:

(Deign to) consume the veil
Which sunders this sweet converse that we hold.

attain to this possession of the union of God through love, wherein all things of the world are denied and renounced, and all the natural affections and appetites are mortified, and the operations of the soul become Divine. All this was broken by the encounters of the soul with this flame when it was oppressive to it; for, in spiritual purgation, as we have said above, the soul succeeds in breaking these two webs and in being united, as it is here, and there remains to be broken only the third web of the life of sense. For this reason the soul here speaks of a web and not of webs; for there is now no other web than this, which, being already so delicate and fine and so greatly spiritualized by this union, is attacked by the flame, not in a rigorous and oppressive way, as were the others, but sweetly and delectably. And thus the death of such souls is ever sweeter and gentler than was their whole life; for they die amid the delectable encounters and impulses of love, like the swan, which sings most sweetly when it is about to die and is at the point of death. For this reason David said: 'Precious is the death of the righteous'; for at such a time the rivers of love of the soul are about to enter the sea, and they are so broad and motionless that they seem to be seas already. The beginning and the end unite together to accompany the righteous man as he departs and goes forth to his kingdom, and praises are heard from the ends of the earth, which are the righteous man's glory.

When, at that time, amid these glorious encounters, the soul feels itself very near to going forth in abundance to the perfect possession of its kingdom, since it sees itself to be pure and rich and prepared to do this, God permits it in this state to see its own beauty and entrusts it with the gifts and virtues that He has given it, and all this turns into love and praise, since there is no leaven to corrupt the mass. And when it sees that it has only now to break the frail web of this human condition of natural life wherein it feels itself to be enmeshed and imprisoned, and its liberty to be impeded, it desires to be loosened and to see itself with Christ, and to burst these bonds of spirit and of flesh,

126

which are of very different natures, so that each may receive its deserts, the flesh remaining upon the earth and the spirit returning to God that gave it. For the flesh profiteth nothing, as St. John says, but has rather been a hindrance to this spiritual good; and the soul grieves that a life which is so high should be obstructed by another that is so low, and therefore begs that this web may be broken.

This life is called a web for three reasons: first, because of the bond that exists between spirit and flesh; second, because it makes a division between God and the soul; third, because even as a web is not so opaque and dense but that the light can shine through it, even so in this state this bond appears to it to be a very fine web, since it is greatly spiritualized and enlightened and refined, so that the Divinity cannot fail to shine through it. And when the soul becomes conscious of the power of the life to come, it also becomes aware of the weakness of this other life, which appears to it as a very fine web—even as a spider's web, which is the name that David gives to it, saying: Our years shall be considered as a spider. And it is much less still in the eyes of a soul that is so greatly enlarged; for, since this soul has entered into the consciousness of God, it is conscious of things in the way that God is; and in the sight of God, as David also says, a thousand years are as yesterday when it is past. And according to Isaiah all nations are as if they were not. And they have the same importance to the soul—namely, all things are to it as nothing, and to its own eyes it is itself nothing: to it its God alone is all.

But here one point should be noticed. Why does the soul beg that the web may be broken, rather than be cut or allowed to wear itself out, since all these things seem to be the same? We may say that there are four reasons. First, in order to use language of greater propriety, for in an encounter it is more proper to say that a thing is broken than that it is cut or wears away. Second, because love delights in the force of love and that of forceful and

127

impetuous contacts, and these express themselves in breaking rather than in cutting or wearing away. Third, because
love desires that the act should be very brief, since it will
then be the more quickly concluded; the briefer and more
spiritual is it, the greater is its power and worth. For virtue
in union is stronger than virtue that is scattered; and love
is introduced as form is introduced into matter, namely,
in an instant, until when there has been no act but only
dispositions for an act; and thus spiritual acts which are
done in an instant are for the most part dispositions of
successive affections and desires, which very rarely succeed
in becoming acts. For this cause the Wise Man said:
Better is the end of a prayer than the beginning. But those
that so succeed instantly become acts in God, for which
reason it is said that the short prayer penetrates the
Heavens. Wherefore the soul that is prepared can perform
more acts and acts of greater intensity in a short time than
the soul that is not prepared can perform in a long time;
for the latter wastes its strength in the preparation of the
spirit, and, even when this is done, the fire has not yet
penetrated the wood. But into the soul that is prepared love
enters continuously, for the spark seizes upon the dry fuel
at its first contact; and thus the soul that is kindled in
love prefers the short act of the breaking of the web to
the long duration of the act of cutting it or of waiting for
it to wear away. The fourth reason is so that the web
of life may the more quickly come to an end, for cutting
a thing and allowing it to wear away are acts performed
after greater deliberation when the thing is riper, and
seem to require more time and a stage of greater maturity,
whereas breaking needs not to wait for maturity or for
anything else of the kind.

And this the soul desires—namely, that it may not have
to wait until its life come naturally to an end nor even to
tarry until it be cut—because the force of love, and the
propensities which it now feels, make it desire and
entreat that its life may be broken by some encounter
and supernatural assault of love. For the soul in this state.

128

knows very well that it is the habit of God to take away such souls before their time in order to give them good things and to take them away from evil things, perfecting them by means of that love in a short time, and giving them that which they might have gained gradually in a long time, even as the Wise Man says, in these words: 'He that is pleasing to God is made beloved, and living among sinners he was translated and taken away, lest malice should affect his understanding or deceit beguile his soul. Being made perfect in a short time, he fulfilled a long time; for his soul was pleasing to God, therefore hasted He to take him out of the midst.' For this reason it is a great thing for the soul to exercise itself greatly in love, so that, when it is perfected here below, it may not stay long, either in this world or the next, before seeing God face to face.

But let us now see why the soul calls this interior assault of the Holy Spirit an encounter rather than by any other name. It is because, as we have said, the soul in God is conscious of an infinite desire that its life may come to an end so that it may have the consummation thereof in glory; yet, because the time is not yet come, this does not happen; and thus, so that the soul may be the more completely perfected and raised up above the flesh, God makes certain assaults upon it that are glorious and Divine and after the fashion of encounters—indeed, they are encounters—wherewith He penetrates the soul continually, deifying its substance and making it Divine. Herein He absorbs the soul, above all being, in the Being of God, for He has encountered it and pierced it to the quick in the Holy Spirit, Whose communications are impetuous when they are full of fervour, as is this communication. This encounter, since it has a lively taste of God, the soul calls sweet; not that many other touches and encounters which it receives in this state are not also sweet and delectable, but rather that this is eminently so above all the rest; for God effects it, as we have said, in order to loose the soul and glorify it. Wherefore the soul takes courage to say: 'Break the web of this sweet encounter.'

And this whole stanza is as though the soul were to say: Oh, flame of the Holy Spirit, that so intimately and tenderly dost pierce the substance of my soul and cauterize it with Thy heat! Since Thou art now so loving as to show that Thou hast the desire of giving Thyself to me in perfect and eternal life; if formerly my petitions failed to reach Thine ears when in their weakness my sense and spirit suffered with yearnings and fatigues of love by reason of the great weakness and impurity and the little strength of love that they had, I entreated Thee to loose me, for with desire did my soul desire Thee when my impatient love would not suffer me to be conformed with the condition of this life that Thou desiredst me to live, and the past assaults of love sufficed not in Thy sight, because they had not sufficient substance; now that I am so greatly strengthened in love that not alone do my sense and spirit not fail before Thee, but rather my heart and my flesh are strengthened in Thy sight, they rejoice in the living God with a close conformity between their various parts. Therefore do I entreat that which Thou desirest me to entreat, and that which Thou desirest not, that desire I not, nor can I desire it, nor does it pass through my mind to entreat it; and, since my petitions are now more effective and more reasonable in Thine eyes (for they go forth from Thee and Thou desirest them, and I pray to Thee with delight and rejoicing in the Holy Spirit, and my judgment comes forth from Thy countenance, which comes to pass when Thou esteemest and hearest my prayers), do Thou break the slender web of this life, and let it not come to pass that age and years cut it after a natural manner, so that I may be able to love Thee with the fullness and satisfaction which my soul desires, without end, for ever.

LIVING FLAME OF LOVE, Stanza I.

GEORGE ALLEN & UNWIN LTD
LONDON: 40 MUSEUM STREET, W.C.1
CAPE TOWN: 58-60 LONG STREET
SYDNEY, N.S.W.: 55 YORK STREET
TORONTO: 91 WELLINGTON STREET WEST
CALCUTTA: 17 CENTRAL AVE., P.O. DHARAMTALA
BOMBAY: 15 GRAHAM ROAD, BALLARD ESTATE
WELLINGTON, N.Z.: 8 KINGS CRESCENT, LOWER HUTT

ETHICAL AND RELIGIOUS CLASSICS OF EAST AND WEST

General Editors

A. J. Arberry, S. Radhakrishnan, H. N. Spalding, F. W. Thomas

In the belief that all the great religions have similarities that confirm and differences that enrich men's spiritual outlook upon the world, a number of eminent scholars have decided to inaugurate a series which will bring out the essentials of religion in this age of doubt and discouragement.

The Series will consist of books of three kinds: translations of imaginative, devotional and philosophic works, with Introduction or Commentary; reproductions of masterpieces of religious art; and Background Books showing the environment in which this literature and art arose and developed. Thus the Series as a whole will seek to bring home to the modern world the highest spiritual achievements of mankind both in East and West.

FIRST TITLES

RUMI, POET AND MYSTIC
by Reynold A. Nicholson

Crown 8vo, 8s. 6d. net

SUFISM
by A. J. Arberry

Crown 8vo, 8s. 6d. net

SAINT FRANCIS IN ITALIAN PAINTING
by George Kaftal

Demy 8vo, 12s. 6d. net

THE POETRY AND CAREER OF LI PO
by Arthur Waley

Crown 8vo, 8s. 6d. net

THE MYSTICS OF SPAIN
by E. Allison Peers

Crown 8vo, about 8s. 6d. net

GEORGE ALLEN AND UNWIN LTD.

Date Due

Date Due			
DEC 16 '52	APR 7 '59		
DEC 19 '52	APR 2 1 '59		
JAN 2 1 '53	MAY 7 '59		
FEB 12 '53	DEC 1 8 '59		
OCT 1 7 '53	MAR 3		
	DEC 13 '61		
OCT 2 8 '53			
SEP 1 6 '54	MR 4 '67		
NOV 2 '55	JY 24 '84		
DEC 2 '55	MEL #: 234442724		
DEC 1 5 '55			
JAN 1 0 '56	Shipped 1/25/18		
OCT 1 1 '56			
MAR 2 2 '57			
APR 1 5 '57			
MAY 6 '57			
MAY 1 3 '57			
AUG 1 0 '58			
JAN 6 '59			
JAN 2 3 '59			

CPSIA information can be obtained
at www.ICGtesting.com
Printed in the USA
BVHW052352080223
658190BV00005B/158